The Complete Guide to Your First Rental Property

A Step-by-Step Plan from the Experts Who Do It Every Day

REVISED 2ND EDITION

First Edition by Teri B. Clark

THE COMPLETE GUIDE TO YOUR FIRST RENTAL PROPERTY: A STEP-BY-STEP PLAN FROM THE EXPERTS WHO DO IT EVERY DAY – REVISED 2ND EDITION

Copyright © 2016 Atlantic Publishing Group, Inc.
1405 SW 6th Avenue • Ocala, Florida 34471 • Phone 800-814-1132 • Fax 352-622-1875
Website: www.atlantic-pub.com •Email: sales@atlantic-pub.com
SAN Number: 268-1250

Library of Congress Cataloging-in-Publication Data

Names: Clark, Teri B., author.
Title: The complete guide to your first rental property : a step-by-step plan
    from the experts who do it every day / Teri B. Clark.
Description: Revised 2nd edition. | Ocala, Florida : Atlantic Publishing
    Group, Inc., [2016] | Includes bibliographical references and index.
Identifiers: LCCN 2016042275 (print) | LCCN 2016050994 (ebook) | ISBN
    9781620230596 (alk. paper) | ISBN 1620230593 (alk. paper) | ISBN
    9781620230756 (ebook-)
Subjects: LCSH: Rental housing--United States--Management. | Real estate
    investment--United States. | Real estate management--United States.
Classification: LCC HD1394.5.U6 C63 2016 (print) | LCC HD1394.5.U6 (ebook) |
    DDC 643/.2--dc23
LC record available at https://lccn.loc.gov/2016042275

Printed in the United States

PROJECT MANAGER AND EDITOR: Rebekah Sack • rsack@atlantic-pub.com
INTERIOR LAYOUT AND JACKET DESIGN: Antoinette D'Amore • addesign@videotron.ca
COVER DESIGN: Meg Buchner • meg@megbuchner.com

Printed on Recycled Paper

Reduce. Reuse.
RECYCLE.

A decade ago, Atlantic Publishing signed the Green Press Initiative. These guidelines promote environmentally friendly practices, such as using recycled stock and vegetable-based inks, avoiding waste, choosing energy-efficient resources, and promoting a no-pulping policy. We now use 100-percent recycled stock on all our books. The results: in one year, switching to post-consumer recycled stock saved 24 mature trees, 5,000 gallons of water, the equivalent of the total energy used for one home in a year, and the equivalent of the greenhouse gases from one car driven for a year.

Over the years, we have adopted a number of dogs from rescues and shelters. First there was Bear and after he passed, Ginger and Scout. Now, we have Kira, another rescue. They have brought immense joy and love not just into our lives, but into the lives of all who met them.

We want you to know a portion of the profits of this book will be donated in Bear, Ginger and Scout's memory to local animal shelters, parks, conservation organizations, and other individuals and nonprofit organizations in need of assistance.

– Douglas & Sherri Brown,
President & Vice-President of Atlantic Publishing

Table of Contents

Foreword

For years, decades even, the American Dream held steady: House in the suburbs. Two-car garage. A white picket fence.

But this being America, that dream did not remain static. We are a country of strivers and climbers. We were founded by people who struck out in the hope — no, in the belief — that they could do more and better than their forbearers. And consistently, we do. This refusal to stand still has helped cement America's place as a haven for those who refuse to settle for what they currently have.

And so the American Dream has evolved. No longer is the house with the two-car garage what we want. Rather, we want to acquire and accumulate wealth in order to obtain a new dream. By obtaining more assets — and not just assets to sit on, but assets we can make work for us — more and more people are achieving the truest of American dreams: passive income.

If you are reading this book, you already know the appeal of passive income. It is the idea that you have money coming in that requires little or no work on your part. What could be better? In particular, you likely understand the added appeal of that passive income coming from a tangible asset such as real estate. Besides the income stream itself, the asset holds "real" value in which you can invest. If that real value can earn a healthy return on an ongoing basis via rental income, all the better.

Now, you are ready to take the plunge. You are ready to move from the American Dream of the 1950s to that of the 21st century. But how to do it? Fortunately, with this book, you have a roadmap. At every step in the process, at every juncture and decision point you will come across, this book pulls from experts across the industry to ensure you have the tools you need to succeed.

One thing that will likely strike you is that it looks like a lot of work. "I thought *passive* was the opposite of active," you are likely thinking. And you are right. Yes, there is a lot of work *on the frontend*. You see, passive income only works when it is set up properly from the beginning. If you don't do the legwork at the start, not only will your income not be passive, but it will likely turn out to be a bad investment overall.

For example, with any real estate investment, the single biggest lever you can pull to make it a "good" or "bad" investment is the price you pay to purchase the real estate. But what is a good price? What is a bad price? To know these things requires you to do your homework; it requires in-depth analysis of the market and trends prior to even looking at an individual property. Do your work at the beginning, and more will fall into place down the line.

One thing you will learn as you work your way through the process is that though there are guiding principles, there is no one-size-fits-all approach to investing and managing rental property. The price points you want to target, the level of activity and engagement you want to maintain throughout the rental process, how many properties you ultimately want to obtain... no book or expert will be able to make those decisions for you. Go in knowing what you want to achieve, and this book will help you achieve it.

In many ways, this is a "Choose Your Own Adventure" book. Like those books, this one can help take you to places you dream about. Unlike those books, this is one for adults who want their dreams achieved in real life, not just on the page.

I would say good luck, but with this book as a guide, you don't need it.

—Andrew McConnell

Andrew McConnell is the Co-Founder and CEO of Rented.com, the first online marketplace that helps owners of rental properties find, compare, and choose the best professional property managers. Andrew holds degrees from Harvard College, Harvard Law School, and Cambridge University, and he has worked with some of the world's largest public and private entities as a management consultant at McKinsey & Co. and as a Director, Solutions Design at Axiom Global, Inc.

Since founding Rented.com, Andrew has focused his attention on one of the fastest growing areas our economy has seen in a number of years: residential rentals. The growth in popularity of platforms like Airbnb and VRBO has created new rental demand and the potential for higher rental incomes than were previously obtainable. At the same time, while many suffered, the dive house prices took coming out of 2008 have made purchasing real estate for the purposes of rental more attractive than ever. The two combined create a once in a generation investment opportunity that Andrew is proud to support and help develop.

Introduction

If you want to build wealth, real estate is one way to do it, and investing in rental property is one of the most popular real estate options today. This is due to the potential rewards as the property appreciates in value, while tenants pay the expenses of the investment.

Of course, any investment has its drawbacks. Managing tenants is a drawback to investing in rental property. Such management includes finding tenants, keeping them, and sometimes evicting them. There are also rules and regulations, state and federal laws, maintenance issues, and rent collections to deal with.

Time is another issue to consider. Rental properties do not create instant wealth, even in strong real estate markets. They are long-term investments with profits coming from the appreciation of property in the market. The money does not come from the actual rental of the property, but from the increase in the value of the real estate over time.

Investing in rental property is not something to enter into lightly. This type of investment involves far more than collecting the rent check each month. To be a successful rental property investor, you do need to understand which properties will appreciate due to location, and you will need to collect those checks, but these things are only one component of success.

Beyond knowledge of the process, you need the mindset it takes to be a real estate investor and landlord. Do you have the time and energy required? Do you have the long-term vision that can get your through the lean times?

Rental property investing takes work. You have to be involved in the process or employ people who are. This type of investing is not like buying a bond and then sitting back and waiting ten years. You will have to be fully committed to owning property as a business venture.

By reading this book, you will acquire the skills you need to:

- Understand the investment aspects of rental properties compared to other investment opportunities
- Understand the basics of being a landlord
- Find available rental homes and choose the right one for you by determining whether the property will make money
- Finance your investment property
- Prepare your property for rent
- Find good tenants
- Manage tenant/landlord issues such as late fees, security deposits, and rental policies

- Determine the repairs that need to be made and the services that need to be offered
- Take advantage of the tax rules and avoid tax mistakes
- Offer a lease option
- Use the computer for your rental property investing
- Retire using your investment funds as income

You will also have access to the landlord tenant laws for all 50 states, documents for closing, word document templates, samples of leases and rental agreements, popular lease clauses, and home maintenance lists.

By the time you finish this book, you will have the knowledge you need to begin investing as a rental property owner. You will also understand what it takes to be a landlord, and you will have the skills and resources necessary to make this form of investing work for you.

Chapter 1

Invest in the Best

Think Long-Term

Each year, some investments are top performers while others fall well short. Real estate can fall into either category depending on the year. Since the recession of 2008, it's fair to say that the residential real estate market has been white-hot. In fact, in many areas, real estate prices are near their all-time highs.

Unlike many investments, real estate is tangible. It is not a piece of paper stating that you own shares, a bond showing that you have given a loan to the government, or a savings account with a receipt showing your money is there. Even money is just paper with a stated value that fluctuates according to currency markets.

Real estate, on the other hand, is something you can see. You are in complete control when it comes to the improvement of your investment, and you determine when your investment property needs to have repairs or additions.

For some, control may not be good. If you prefer ease over control, then rental property investing is not for you.

The Past and the Future

One big draw of real estate is that it tends to offer a secure and steady return on investment (ROI), even in times of uncertainty. As of 2016, the United States economy had firmly shook off the Great Recession of 2008–2009 and was growing at a steady, though not spectacular, growth rate. Local real estate markets certainly benefitted.

A big factor is population. The population of the United States will continue to grow well into the future, albeit at a slower growth rate compared with previous decades. It will also become considerably more grey and diverse. Consider these trends:

- The U.S. population is expected to increase from 319 million to 400 million in 2051.
- One in five Americans is expected to be 65 years old or more by 2033. In the next 30 years, people over the age of 65 will double to 70 million.
- Latinos will account for three-fourths of labor force growth by 2020, according to the Bureau of Labor Statistics (BLS).

With population growth comes people getting married, having babies, and finding new jobs as well as retiring, downsizing, and generally easing into their Golden Years. All this generates the need for new housing, which will likely keep the market vibrant and present some intriguing investment options.

Understanding the demographics might lead you to purchase single story homes to accommodate people over 55 or smaller homes to attract the single person household. You may decide that purchasing in a city or perhaps a walkable suburban community is a good idea. Of course, all demographic trends will need to be gauged against the specific geographic area in which you intend to invest.

Demographics can certainly also help you choose geographic locations. For instance, the Latino population will migrate mostly from Mexico, so border states will be growing. Looking at the aging population, you can assume that the Sunbelt states will grow as people in the northern states retire to a warmer climate.

Due to current population trends, real estate will likely remain strong well into the future.

There are many other rules relating to IRA real estate holdings. It is best to contact a lawyer well-versed in IRA real estate tax laws.

INVESTOR INSIGHT:

Investing in real estate is always a good idea, as long as you are doing so long term. Investing in rental properties is good, even in times of a downward trend, because even those who cannot afford to buy will need a place to live and renting a home is a good option.

Retire With Property

Building a retirement nest egg is one reason why people buy real estate. It is now possible to buy real estate using retirement funds in your IRA or

401(k). To do so, you have to put your funds, or roll them over, into a self-directed IRA. A self-directed IRA allows you to make the financial decisions instead of leaving them to someone else, like a manager of a mutual fund.

Real estate held this way needs to be for the long term. You will get the benefits of the appreciation of your assets, but you will not be able to live off rental income until you have reached the age of 65 ½ without taking penalty losses. You will also be unable to deduct depreciation since the investment is not taxable. The increase in principle, however, will hopefully be enough to offset the negative aspects of holding real estate in an IRA.

It is imperative to know the rules regarding holding real estate in an IRA. Not knowing them can be devastating to you in fines and in taxes.

For instance, you are allowed to purchase any kind of property with an IRA fund as long as you do not use that property for yourself. You may purchase a beach home as an investment property, but may not use it two weeks a year. After you retire, you can take the house out of your IRA as a distribution and use it any way you would like, but while it is in the IRA, you may not use it.

There is also the matter of who you may rent the property to. You cannot rent to your spouse or your direct ascendants or descendants, such as grandparents or children, but you can rent to your siblings, aunts, uncles, and cousins.

INVESTOR INSIGHT:

There are many other rules relating to IRA real estate holdings. It is best to contact a lawyer well-versed in IRA real estate tax laws.

CASE STUDY: CHRIS LENGQUIST

Chris Lengquist
Keller Williams Realty
Ad Astra Realty
www.adastrarealty.com
913-322-7500
Twitter: @Chrislengquist

Chris Lengquist, a real estate investor in the Kansas City area, believes that real estate is always a good investment. When asked why, he gives the following reasons:

- It is easily accessible to a wide variety of investors of all ages.
- Real estate can be leveraged.
- People know their neighborhood and the housing in their area and can capitalize on this knowledge.
- Over the long-haul, you cannot lose money with real estate.
- You get cash flow before taxes.

For Chris, it is also rewarding. "I take a certain amount of pride knowing that not only am I securing a retirement for me and my wife, but I am providing clean, safe, and affordable housing to those not able or willing to purchase their own home."

Chris believes that buying a home is a solid move, even during a downturn.

"There simply is no "wrong time" to buy. If the property meets your credentials, then buy it. If you never buy because it is always the wrong time, you will end up with nothing in the end. Act now!"

Although he only currently owns two properties, his goal is 10 to 14. Having this number of properties will meet the financial goals he has set. "I invest for growth, not cash flow. Any cash flow I get goes right back into the operating account. My pay-off is down the road." How many rentals you own, either more or less, will completely depend on your financial goals and abilities as an investor.

"To me, a good mix is three to four multi-family homes to every six or seven single family homes. I have no problem with one in Kansas City, one in Tulsa, and one in Baton Rouge, as long as the home will pay for itself and its property manager."

According to Chris, knowing whether a property is a good rental property is simple. Simply ask yourself, "Will it make money?"

First, you have to know what ROI goals you are shooting for. You need to look at cash flow, principal reduction, depreciation, and appreciation. Then you can determine whether the property will give you those returns.

Be diligent in your pursuit of properties to find those that fit your criteria, such as location, type of property, or number of bedrooms. In addition to finding a property with the right criteria, you will need to see whether the goals you wish to reach can be reached in a timely manner. You will also need to look at the cash you have on hand. A professional real estate agent and/or counselor can help you.

Chris says, "On your first deal or two, do not try to do it alone. Have someone with experience walk you through, and do not pick any old agent. Find one that knows real estate investing."

When a property fits, you need to finance it. "Leveraging your money means using other people's money. Whether it is a bank, a mortgage broker, or a private lender, you sell them on the investment and your real estate capabilities and you use their money for the bulk of the transaction."

Finding tenants can be difficult. Chris says, "I think I scare off quite a few prospective tenants, but I would rather be empty another month than get a bad tenant."

Here is his strategy:

- Make polite conversation peppered with questions that let you know who they are, where they work, and why they are moving.

- Tell them that you keep your units in good condition and expect them to do the same.

- Tell them that you will be in every 60 to 90 days to verify that the property does not have any new water leaks or other problems.

- Inform them that you are an observant landlord and will be involved in the property.

These techniques may make some tenants disappear, but Chris has found that he is quite happy with those who are willing to stick around.

Chris is involved in the maintenance and upkeep of his properties. "I expect much from my tenants and I tell them so. So in return I turn over to them a unit that is clean, safe, freshly painted, and with clean carpeting. I do not rent a house with known defects. If they find one, they can call me right away and I will fix it. However, they know that if they did it, they fix it."

He watches the properties closely and goes through each property at least once every 90 days, even if it is just to replace a furnace filter.

"This gives me a chance to see how the property is being cared for. If I do not like something I see, I can take care of it then and there. I do not want to walk into a property after 12 to 24 months and find out the dog has been urinating on the carpet, the kids have been carving into the walls, and that the pipe under the bathroom sink has a slow leak."

Although Chris uses a lease drawn up by his attorney, he has this to say concerning leases: "I am a believer that if a tenant gets the urge to jump, they will. A lease is not going to do much good, unless I want to spend my time and my money tracking them down to sue them."

What has been Chris's best experience in the world of rental investments? "Any time a house does not hold a nasty surprise, it is a best experience. Do your homework, get inspections, and check the numbers two and three times. Do all that and you will find most experiences to be pleasant."

More Than One Way to Invest

Real estate investing can take many forms. Let us look at the options.

Speculation

When you invest in spec homes, you are buying a home with the expectation that the home will rise in value. To get the most appreciation, the investor buys low and sells high. Straightforward speculation investing means buying homes off the market or homes that are in the process of being built. These homes have no particular problems or issues, but you feel that the sale price is low and that you have the opportunity to sell at a higher price.

One advantage to investing in the speculation market is quick profit realization. If you time it right, you can make a good deal of money in just one year, especially if you were able to finance with a low down payment and you have many properties. This method of investing is common when times are good. The market can change suddenly, and if you have many properties that are not appreciating quickly enough, you can find yourself with expenses far exceeding any profits you could make.

INVESTOR INSIGHT:

With speculation investing, you can plan to lose money each month. The key is that you believe, or speculate, that you will make that money back and more when you sell.

There are some ways to make this form of investing less risky. Look for job creation in the area. As jobs are created, housing demands increase. If, however, the job boom is not evident in your area, a national housing boom will not affect you, and you are likely to lose money.

You can also watch interest rates. Falling rates mean that homes are more affordable, giving you a better chance of having someone able to buy your home.

Finally, look at the boom of local fast food chains. Before restaurants such as McDonald's come into an area, market demographics are scrutinized. If there is not sufficient population or expected growth, new restaurants will not come.

Speculation is a risky way to invest in real estate. If you do not have the money to lose each month until you sell, or the money to hang on during the downward trends, then speculation is not a wise investment option for you.

Investing in seized property

Investing in seized property is similar to speculation. The main difference is that with seized property, you have a far better chance of buying at a low price. Homes are seized when taxes are owed and have not been paid. The property is then sold off for the taxes, fines, and interest, or it is sold at auction.

Before purchasing a seized property, you need to find out:

- Whether the property is worth more than the taxes owed
- How the property is zoned
- What the state and local laws are concerning the rights of the previous owner

Like speculation properties, your hope is that you will buy low and sell high. The same pitfalls of speculation properties are attached to investing in seized property.

Fixer-uppers

A fixer-upper home is one that needs a number of repairs and renovations to be of similar value to the homes around it. If you invest in a fixer-upper, you intend to buy the distressed house at a low price, fix it up, and then sell it at a premium price.

Fixer-uppers are another kind of speculative venture. Taking a distressed home and making it a home that lives up to the standards of the neighborhood can be costly. It also involves making the assumption that you are going to be able to bring the house up to the standard required.

One way to lessen the risk of the speculative nature of this kind of investing is to have more than one fixer-upper property. This way, if one property loses money, you have another to make up that loss.

The heavy taxes on gains are another disadvantage. Each time you sell a home, you have to pay a capital gains tax. Since the home will not be your primary residence, the entire tax will be due even if you use the profits to buy a home of higher value.

Live in it and then sell it

One way to invest in real estate is to buy a home, live in it while fixing it up, and then sell it. As long as you live in the home for at least two years, it will be considered your primary residence, and capital gains will be eliminated.

Since you plan to live on site, you are more likely to have done your homework concerning the location. Once again, you need to buy low. The best way to buy low is to look for a home that does not quite meet the standards of the surrounding neighborhood.

A home may be just below the standards of the surrounding neighborhood due to:

- Low-end kitchen
- Inadequate number of bathrooms
- Small closets

- Lack of landscaping
- Out of date woodwork, wallpaper, color scheme, or appliances

If you are willing to live in a house undergoing renovations, this strategy may be a good way to invest. The biggest risk involved is that you end up putting more money into the home than you can get out of it. The major benefit of this kind of investment is that while you are selling, you are living in the home, which means that you are deriving a benefit while the home is on the market.

Private mortgage investing

A private mortgage happens when you loan private money to an individual buying a home, and this borrower cannot meet the requirements for a conventional loan. These loans are short-term (six months to three years) loans based on the value of the property instead of the borrower's credit.

The advantages to private mortgage investing are many:

- High interest rate on your investment
- Monthly income
- Secure investment — as long as you have done your homework on the true value of the home

Before investing in a mortgage, you need to understand the loan-to-value ratio, which is not as technical as it sounds. It is the ratio of the loan on the mortgage compared to the value of the mortgage, and it is found by dividing the loan by the mortgage value.

For example, if you loan $70,000 on a $100,000 house, your loan-to-value (LTV) is 70 percent. If you only loaned $50,000, then your LTV would be 50 percent. The lower your LTV, the safer your investment. Most successful private mortgage investors do not loan out more than a 70 percent LTV.

Whenever you decide to lend money privately on a mortgage, it is imperative that you check out the property yourself. The home may be located in an area that has a good reputation, but that should not be enough for you. The house may be rundown or it may be far smaller than you were led to believe. The house may also be poorly located within a good neighborhood — i.e., next to the community dump or a loud rollerblading park.

INVESTOR INSIGHT:

You are lending money, and your money will be safe if your loan-to-value ratio is not more than 70 percent. The only way you can know this for sure is to see the home yourself.

Although private mortgage investing is a good way to invest, there are some associated cons. As with other real estate investing, it is not a liquid investment because you will have agreed to lend the money for a specified time. Additionally, you have to have at least $10,000 to invest to get started, and higher amounts will provide you with far more choices.

Real estate stocks

Another way to invest in real estate is through a Real Estate Investment Trust (REIT). A REIT is a fund — one that is very similar to a standard mutual fund — that invests in real estate, usually income-producing real estate. There are two basic types of REITs. Equity REITs purchase commercial real estate and then lease the properties to commercial tenants. Mortgage REITs invest in mortgage-backed securities, both residential and commercial. And then there are so-called hybrid REITs. These REITs invest in two ways — directly in real estate properties and in mortgage-backed securities.

You can invest in an equity REIT that focuses on only one type of property or on a variety of properties. Some possible property investments include:

- Apartments
- Hotels
- Medical buildings
- Warehouses
- Offices
- Mobile home parks
- Public self-storage
- Regional malls
- Shopping centers
- Factory outlets
- Restaurants
- Golf courses

With an REIT, you can build a diverse portfolio quickly. You can also get started with little investment.

There are, of course, drawbacks to investing in an REIT. An REIT can underperform in relation to the stock market. Additionally, the tax rate on REIT income does not qualify for the lower federal rate on dividends. Rather, these investors pay taxes at the ordinary income tax rate.

Rental Diversity

There is more than one way to invest in rental properties. You can invest in:

- Rental homes
- Rent-to-own homes
- Low income rentals
- Boarding homes
- Commercial real estate

All these options have differing pros and cons. For instance, a rental home is a reliable long-term investment. The same holds true with low-income housing, but you may find that you have more repair and tenant issues. With boarding homes, you will have the headache of large turnovers since those who rent only a room are often more transient than those who rent a home. Finally, when renting commercial real estate, you have to worry about long vacancies, often for a year at a time.

All these options require many of the same skills from you. To be an investor of rental property, you become the landlord and must obtain the necessary skills.

Chapter 2

So, You Want To Be a Landlord?

Just a Landlord?

If you own commercial or private property and agree to rent it to someone else, you become a landlord. Every person renting out property is a landlord of some type, whether it is a small one-man operation or a multimillion-dollar operation with Donald Trump at the head.

Many people want to be a landlord to bring in the rent money every month and benefit from the increasing housing prices, but being a landlord is not that simple.

To be a landlord, you have to:

- Fill vacancies as quickly as possible

- Know and follow the laws regarding rental properties
- Make repairs on your properties as necessary
- Provide a safe dwelling, also known as a habitable condition, for your tenants
- Determine rent charges and collect them
- Find good tenants and keep them
- Deal with difficult tenants
- Keep accurate records of applications, rent payments, agreements, notices, purchases, repairs, maintenance, and services
- File taxes
- Maintain insurance on the properties

Though the drawbacks of becoming a landlord are many, so are the benefits. For instance, you can create a stream of income that supports your investment and may even provide you with monthly income for living expenses. While you earn this income, your investment will continue to appreciate as long as it is maintained properly, so you can see profits in the long-term.

To be a landlord, you have to determine whether the benefits of owning the property outweigh the risks and annoyances involved.

What Is Your Type?

There are three main types of landlords: owner/occupant, absentee, and property manager. Determining which type you want to be will depend on your investment goals, your time, your knowledge, and your desire to be directly involved in the day-to-day operations of your rental properties.

Owner-occupant landlord

An owner-occupant landlord lives in the property being rented. An owner-occupant landlord situation is possible with any multi-tenant situation, such as an apartment building. If you choose to live on your investment property, you will find that your tenants expect immediate service when they have a problem. Landlording becomes a 24/7 job.

There are also many good aspects of being an owner-occupant. Even a responsible tenant is not likely to keep the yard picked up or the unit clean as well as the owner of the property. Rather than have an investment that is "out of sight, out of mind," owner-occupants constantly have the investment placed before them and will strive to keep up the conditions.

Absentee landlord

This term has bad connotations, but simply means that the owner does not live on the premises. An absentee landlord can live one block away or several states away. Many absentee landlords check out their property on a regular basis and, although they cannot make immediate changes like an owner-occupant, they keep their property in good shape and deal with their tenants on a regular basis.

INVESTOR INSIGHT:

It is true that some absentee landlords are truly absent except when it is time to collect a rent check. If you wish to be absent from the process, the best thing for you to do is to hire a property manager.

Property manager

A property manager is a type of landlord who is paid by the owner of the property. For a set fee, the property manager can do the following:

- Rent or lease apartments
- Hire contractors to make repairs
- Collect rents
- Return deposits
- Find tenants
- Evict tenants
- Keep accounting records

If you do not wish to be involved in the day-to-day workings of rental investments, this type of landlord arrangement may be right for you.

❧ *Been There, Done That* ☙

Investor and business advisor Carol Sankar explains that while screening tenants is a good idea, many forget the importance of vetting property managers as well. She owned and operated a group of single-family properties when she learned about the importance of "limiting" her availability to tenants.

She explains, "Before I learned how to effectively use a property management service, I thought all landlords had to convene with tenants. However, my biggest mistake was trusting the *wrong* property manager." She had a property that was vacant for some time, and her property manager, who she admits was not correctly vetted, rented the home to a group of ladies without Carol's knowledge and was collecting rent without remittance.

Carol recalls, "He scammed over $10,000 from the tenants between the deposit and unpaid rent. The tenants were furious and began to believe that I was a part of the scam. However, we all later found his picture on the front of the newspaper after he was arrested for fraud."

Team Spirit

Investing in real estate does not need to be a lone-wolf venture. You are going to do much better if you have a team you can trust. Team members will each bring their own expertise to the table to help you be successful.

Possible team members include:

1. Bank broker or mortgage lender: A broker can help you with many different financing options. A lender is the one who makes the loan decision and can give you pre-approval. It will be up to you to determine which you want on your team. You may decide that you want both.

INVESTOR INSIGHT:

If you choose a mortgage lender, you may want to develop a relationship with someone in a small town community bank. Small banks are more flexible and can offer choices that larger banks do not have the decision-making power to give.

Whichever you choose, they are likely to have good relationships with realtors in your area, which brings us to the next team member on the list.

2. Real estate agent: An agent who is experienced in your area of investment is a good addition to your team. The agent will have access to the Multiple Listing Service and will know, often before you do, when something of interest to you is for sale.

To find a good agent, ask around. Your banker may know of someone, but so may your friends. Referrals from people you trust is the main way people find agents. That said, you can always search for agents online with simple searches. Many agents offer web pages chock full of information. No matter what, you should always interview several agents until you feel comfortable with one. In the beginning, you may choose to work with three or four until you determine which one best suits your needs.

3. Attorney: You do not want just any attorney, but a real estate attorney. You want someone who knows the real estate laws in your area and can help you close your deals quickly and easily. Since you will be buying rentals, you also will want your attorney to know about leases, tenant/landlord laws, evictions, and other items unique to rental property.

4. Real Estate Accountant: The IRS has hundreds of laws, deductions, and penalties that change every year. Having a good accountant who is well-versed in real estate finances is imperative.

5. Real Estate Appraiser: An appraiser is trained to give an estimate of the worth of a property. They will provide you with a detailed report that will be used by your mortgage lender to determine the amount of money that can be loaned on the property. A fair appraiser will know if you are getting a good deal and will get you the financing you need.

6. Inspector: Before purchasing a piece of property, you will want to have it inspected. Sometimes, a home that looks good to the novice is not good.

Structural defects, outdated wiring, and poor plumbing may go unnoticed. An inspector can help you see what repairs need to be made and then you can determine whether the property meets your investment criteria.

7. Contractor: No matter what type of property you buy, there will be repairs to make either at the time of purchase or after a tenant leaves. These repairs may be large or small, but unless you are handy with tools and want to spend your time on maintenance, having a reliable contractor is a good addition to your team. In the beginning, you may need to try several different contractors until you find one who gives you reasonable and accurate quotes, gets the work done in a reasonable time, and is reliable.

INVESTOR INSIGHT:

Having an inspector who is also a contractor can be quite valuable. This person will be able to tell you about the problems and the cost of repairs.

Investor Insight: Having an inspector who is also a contractor can be quite valuable. This person will be able to tell you about the problems and the cost of repairs.

8. Property Manager: A final person you may want on your team is a property manager. Since this position requires full-time involvement in your investment business, the next section details what a property manager is and how to hire one.

You Invest, They Manage

If you choose not to be involved in the day-to-day operations of your business, you will need to hire a property manager. You can either pay a company to do the work or hire an independent manager.

If you hire a company, you are contracting out the work; the management company is an expense but the actual property manager is not considered your employee. But if you hire an independent manager, you are hiring an employee and will be responsible for filing paperwork with the IRS and assuming responsibility for any actions taken by the manager.

Property management company

Here are a few things to look for when hiring a property management company:

1. **Fees:** Fees are derived in one of two ways — percentage fee or flat fee. The percentage fee is the most common and can be anywhere from five to 20 percent of the money your property brings in. You need to look for a reputable company that provides the most services for the least amount of money.

2. **Contact:** Consider whether the management company will be responsive to your calls, whether they use email or have after-hour availability to you, and how quickly they will respond to you. You need to deal with a company that is personable and cares about you and your needs. Your investment is at stake, and you want someone who shows his or her concern toward you.

3. **Contract:** Find out whether there are charges or penalties to terminate your contract in case things are not working out.

4. **Property Maintenance:** There are several questions to ask a management company regarding maintenance:

   • Who does the maintenance on the property?
   • Do they have their own crew?
   • What do they charge you per hour for maintenance?

- What kinds of repairs do they handle?
- What do they do if a repair comes about that they do not handle?
- How much will they spend without contacting you?
- Do they provide invoices and/or receipts for expenses due to repairs and maintenance?

INVESTOR INSIGHT:

You will want to set a limit on what the management company may spend without contacting you. For many investors, $100 is a good set point.

5. **Statements:** Find out how often the company sends out income/expense statements. These are often sent monthly or quarterly, but monthly statements make it easier for you to determine whether the fees are what you expected and allow you to make quicker decisions concerning the management company.

6. **Tenant problems:** Find out how the management company handles evictions and whether this will be at an additional cost to you. Ask whether they have experienced legal counsel within their company to handle evictions.

7. **Yard work:** Determine whether yard work is part of the management company's responsibilities. Ask about the costs of yard work, landscaping, and snow removal.

8. **Reserves:** Management companies require that you put up a certain amount of money in reserve in case anything comes up quickly. You will want to find out how much money the company will require you to put into the reserve fund.

9. **Accounting:** Find out how often the management company sends a check to you and whether they put tenant deposits into an escrow account.

10. **Advertising:** Advertising will need to be done to fill vacancies. Find out where and how the management company advertises.

INVESTOR INSIGHT:

According to the National Association of REALTORS®, 42 percent of home buyers' first step in their search was to look at homes online, while 14 percent first contacted an agent.

You will also want to ask general questions such as:

- How many managers do they employ?
- How many properties do they manage?
- What types of rental properties do they focus on?

- How long have they been in business?
- Do they have referrals that you may contact?

Finding a good property management company will help you leave the day-to-day issues of real estate investing behind. You should constantly evaluate the relationship with your company and change companies as you feel necessary.

❈ *Been There, Done That* ❧

Andrew McConnell urges even rental owners who think that they are taking all the cautionary steps necessary to look into using the services of Rented.com to help them find a good, local property manager.

An owner of a rental condo in Panama City Beach in Florida was tired of dealing with college students during the boisterous spring break season. The beach is popular with students who want to use their break to party as much as possible, so the owner decided that the only solution was simply not to rent his property during that time. That way, he would certainly avoid broken windows, spills on carpets, holes in the walls, and anything else that drunk partiers are capable of.

But, on his own, he couldn't stop the chaos of spring break season from entering his condo. A group of drunk renters mistook his condo for theirs. After several attempts to unlock the door with the key from their similar condo on a nearby floor, they broke down his door in a drunken attempt to access their vacation home!

A property manager would have helped him to monitor his condo and helped to deal with the damage.

Independent property manager

When hiring an independent manager, you will need to determine what their job will entail.

- Will they select tenants?
- Will they resolve day-to-day problems?
- Will they maintain the property?
- Will they hire contractors?
- Will they make small repairs themselves?
- Will they collect rent?
- Will they evict tenants?

You will have to determine how much you plan to pay your employee. As with a management company, you have several options. You can give your employee a salary, pay by the hour, or pay a percentage.

If you have a multi-tenant property, you will also need to determine whether the property manager will live on the property. While common, this practice is not a necessity. Many real estate investors who hire a property manager include free rent for the unit as part of the salary.

As you interview potential employees, you will want to look at their previous experience and, if required by state law, whether the candidate possesses a current license. You will also want to check their references. The manager will need to be familiar with Fair Housing Laws, basic landlord-tenant laws, accounting practices, the internet, and basic maintenance.

INVESTOR INSIGHT:

Do not simply collect their references. Check them out. Ask questions about their experience, personality, and style. If you just ask whether they were a good employee, you are likely to get a "yes" answer but no real information.

Some questions you may consider asking during an interview to hire an independent property manager include:

- Tell me about your past experience. What did you like most about your last job? What did you like the least?
- Do you have experience collecting rent?
- Do you have experience doing general repairs?
- What kinds of problems have you resolved in the past? How did you resolve them?
- What about this job interests you?

After you have interviewed the applicant and checked their references, you will need to do a credit history and background check. Your property manager will be handling money with no direct supervision. Someone with poor personal finances may not handle the money correctly or may be more inclined to steal. The background check will give you information on their character, reputation, and lifestyle.

INVESTOR INSIGHT:

You must obtain the applicant's consent to check their credit and background by using a form with their signature and date. If they refuse these checks, do not consider them for the position.

Depending on your needs, hiring an independent property manager may be the best option for your investment goals. Whether you hire a company or an individual, you are the owner of the property, and it is up to you to do what is best for your tenants. If you do not like what you see with the management of your property, make the necessary changes.

⊗ Been There, Done That ⊗

Andrew McConnell tells the happy story of how John B., owner of a property in Denver, Colorado, began making more money when his property became a short-term rental and when he hired the assistance of a property management company.

John B. purchased his second home in Denver in 2009. Shortly afterward, he realized that he needed some extra income, so he decided to rent out the property on a year-long lease.

He was happy with his renter, and he liked the stability of having a long-term tenant, but because of the rise of sites like Airbnb, he knew that he could supplement his income more if he rented out his house on a short-term basis.

When his tenant left, he created a listing on Airbnb. Everything worked out smoothly at first. His home was in a neighborhood that visitors to Denver liked to frequent. He used a local cleaning service, but took the time to manage marketing, bookkeeping, some cleaning, and other maintenance himself. Since he lived outside of Denver, he also made the effort to travel to his property every four months to see how it was faring.

His first year as a short-term renter was somewhat of a success. He had hosted 100 guests and made $46,000. But after the expenses for cleaning and maintenance, he was only making $34,000.

He began to wonder about finding a property manager and decided to use Rented.com to help him find one. They could connect him with more than 550 potential management companies and help him weigh competing offers.

After weighing a few companies, he found a management company who guaranteed him $39,600 a year, while taking care of all of the work that he had been doing. John explains, "Being able to be completely hands off and having the money guaranteed is really nice."

After you understand the role of a landlord and make your decision to become one, it is time to think about the property you will buy. In Chapter 3, we will explore how to find the right rental home for you.

Seek and Ye Shall Find

s you look at rental properties, you will notice that the process takes plenty of time, a network of people, and knowledge. Jumping in without the proper base is a recipe for disaster.

Wait, Do Not Seek Yet

Before you even begin looking at a property, there are some things you must consider first.

Look at the time

Consider how long you plan to own a rental property. The longer you own, the more appreciation you will earn in the end, but you will also be investing in more repairs, maintenance, and improvements.

If you plan to keep a home for 10 years and the home is five years old, you most likely will not have to put on a new roof or buy new appliances. On the other hand, if you plan to keep the same home for 20 years, you are likely to have to replace the roof and the major appliances. If you only plan to keep a home for a short time, you will want to buy a property that will not need major repairs unless you believe you can recoup the cost of them.

Another thing to consider is the appreciation of the home. If you keep a home for 20 years, the appreciation on the property will be high. If you plan to sell in five years, you will need to make more money on the minimal appreciation in that time and a bigger annual return through higher rents to make the purchase worthwhile.

INVESTOR INSIGHT:

For most small investors, long-term property investing is the wisest choice, because it allows them to remain unscathed during market dips.

Networks count

Developing a network is a good way to find properties that are available. Trying to find one on your own is not as easy, because the good ones may be snatched up quickly by those "in the know."

As you get started, you will want to join local landlord associations, property owner associations, real estate groups, and chamber groups. These groups will help you find out what is for sale. As you become more known in these circles, people with deals will come looking for you instead of you having to do all the searching.

Another method is to approach a landlord directly to see if they want to sell their property. You will be surprised by the number of landlords who are ready to get out of the business.

Money matters

You are going to need a loan to get started on your real estate investing venture. To get an excellent loan, you will need an excellent credit rating. If your credit rating is poor, you will need bigger down payments, and you will receive higher interest rates.

Additionally, when applying for a loan for a rental unit, the bank or other mortgage lender will want to see the financial balance sheet. If your credit is poor, this balance sheet will have to be much stronger than the normal requirement.

To get a better credit rating, pay down your credit cards and consumer debt, and pay all your bills on time. Doing these two things will increase your credit score in a matter of six to 12 months.

You are also going to need a cash reserve beyond the down payment needed when buying the property. This cash reserve is for unexpected repairs, maintenance, and vacancies. The money you owe the bank is due whether you have a tenant or not. If your unit is vacant for two months, you will need to have the money to make the mortgage payment without a tenant's rent.

INVESTOR INSIGHT:

The rule of thumb is that you set aside at least one month's rent for each unit. You may also consider having a line of credit to cover large costs.

In the know

When it comes to real estate investing, knowledge is imperative.

If you overpay, you will have a much tougher time recouping your initial investment, and you will never make as much as you could have if you had made a better deal. Real estate investing has to be practical. If you let your emotions take over, you will be blind to bad deals. Stick to the numbers. Falling in love with a piece of property is investor suicide.

Ensuring that rental income will cover your costs is key. These costs include:

- Mortgage payment on the property
- Taxes
- Insurance
- Maintenance
- Repairs
- Vacancy rate

INVESTOR INSIGHT:

The typical vacancy rate is five percent. If you have one unit for twelve months and multiply that by five percent, you can expect to have the unit empty half a month each year or one month every two years.

Now that you know the basics, the goal of finding an investment property can be realized.

✎ *Been There, Done That* ✎

Dawn Cook, real estate agent and home stager in Indiana, shares what she looks for in a rental property and why:

Price is first for us, then area, and then the condition of the place.

Price is always most important to us. If we do not get a good price, then it might not be worth it to us to rent it out. We always keep in mind the option of selling, so we need a nice margin of profit in that area as well. I feel a property should always be able to pay for itself, plus extra for our pocket and for any future problem that may arise.

Location is key. If the property is in an undesirable area, you may have a problem obtaining renters and keeping them. Finally, we look at the physical shape of the property. We do not want to put much work into the place to get it ready to rent. It is a blessing to put that for rent sign up and start the ad in the paper on the day of closing.

We prefer one bedroom units because they are for one to two people. This way, we do not have to deal with multiple people in and out regarding wear and tear on the property. It also eliminates multiple vehicles and we get, in our opinion, more money in return.

We see it as this: The more people in a property, the higher likelihood of problems and issues that will take up our time and possibly our money. In the past we have had excellent experiences with one-bedroom places. They are quickly rented with minimal headaches.

Location, Location, Location

If you have been around real estate in any way, you have heard that the three most important factors when buying real estate are location, location, location. Location is important when dealing with rental properties. Without the proper location, you will not be able to earn enough tenant income to pay your monthly bills.

The problem lies in the fact that there is no one right location. It depends on your particular area and your investment goals.

If you want to invest in a busy city, units that are close to public transportation and city amenities, such as restaurants and theaters, will be in the right location. On the other hand, if you are buying in a suburban neighborhood, a unit near a shopping center and local park and in a good school district makes more sense.

If you are buying vacation rentals, a home on the beach is preferable to one a block from the ocean. A lakefront property will bring you higher rent than one that simply has a view of the lake.

If your rentals will be for working families, buying property in areas with many jobs or in easy commuting distance of a bigger city will be essential. Working families will also want grocery stores nearby, local daycare centers, and activities such as soccer and scouting.

When checking out the location, you will want to walk through the area on several different occasions and at several different times of the day. While you are looking around, ask yourself whether you would feel comfortable living here as a renter.

Other questions to consider are:

- How is the neighborhood kept up? Are the homes taken care of and is the yard work being done?
- What kind of amenities are in the area? Are there shopping centers, grocery stores, parks, jogging trails, restaurants, and is there access to local transit?
- Is the school system good? Does the school offer after-school care?
- Are there sidewalks, parks, and playgrounds for children to play?
- Does the property have a fenced yard for children and pets?
- How easy is it to access the interstate or other main routes into and out of town?
- Is the property close to you?

As you start your rental business, having your properties close at hand will make the whole process easier. If you look for properties near your home, you will be better able to answer all the questions about the neighborhood. It will also be easier to find the help you need, such as repair work, by using someone you already know and trust.

Houses, Apartments, Condos, Oh My

In addition to location, you must consider the type of property you wish to purchase. City dwellers want to be near city amenities, but they also want something easy to take care of. Those in the city do not tend to want yards. Condominiums or apartments would fit this description.

If you are considering buying homes for the working class, you need to think about families. Most families want three bedrooms, a garage, and a yard, suggesting single-family homes or a duplex. Single renters or young couples are looking for two bedrooms and often do not care as much about a yard, suggesting a duplex, a townhome, or an apartment building.

Even if you decide to buy single-family homes, there are more decisions to make. Do you want one, two, three, or four bedrooms? Do you want a garage, a carport, or no protection for a vehicle? Do you want a yard? Will the yard be fenced? Do you want a deck or patio? Do you want one story or two? Do you want a home with a basement? What about a workshop or storage shed?

To figure out these details, you need to figure out who your tenants will be by looking at your area and examining the market.

⊗ *Been There, Done That* ⊗

Whitney Nicely, principal broker at Whitney Buys Houses, LLC, which is based in Tennessee, loves to buy raw pieces of land. Some of her best deals have come from the local county's tax sale. One day in March not too long ago, she went to the courthouse to buy some properties, having prepared an Excel spreadsheet of the ones she wanted and having taken the time to drive by and look at her favorite options.

Finally, an attorney called out the lot number that she had been waiting for. Eagerly, she wrote down the parcel ID. He said the number wrong, but she knew — or thought she knew — that this was her longed-for property. After all, he said Douglas Lake, and that was what she wanted.

As Whitney recounts, "The opening bid was $400. *Sweet,* I thought, presuming that I must have written down the amount wrong. I had thought it would start at $3,000."

She swiftly raised her hand. Since the attorney wasn't an auctioneer, the wait for the next bid took a long time. Someone finally bid $450.

Whitney decided she was in for $500, and, surprisingly, the other bidder shook his head no.

She was delighted, believing that she had won the "whole 15 acres overlooking Douglas Lake… for a measly $500!"

But when she went to pay her bill for that property and a few other finds, she heard the clerk laughing that someone actually bought Lot #6. Whitney informed her that she won Lot #6. She giggled again and sarcastically told her that she had made a great investment.

Whitney was bewildered. Certainly people should be congratulating her on her great investment! Wouldn't everyone love this beautiful lakefront property?

Then, she realized that the receipt had the same parcel ID that she had thought was incorrect when the attorney rambled it off.

She rummaged through newspaper clippings to see if she had indeed made a mistake. Then, she looked at her Excel spreadsheet. Trying desperately to get an internet connection, she searched for the parcel ID on her phone's browser.

Eventually, it became apparent that she had bought five acres *under* Douglas Lake. There were no trees, no grass, no building site, no dock permits, no potential back porch or grilling area, and no way to watch the sun set over the mountains.

After this experience, Whitney has some advice for fellow buyers of properties: "Double check parcel numbers when doing your due diligence. Then, have your assistant triple check your work."

Nevertheless, Whitney jokingly suggests a few potential ideas for the property: installing an underground houseboat and draping a bright pink "Whitney Buys Houses" banner on the side.

How Much?

How much you are willing to spend on your investment property will depend on your credit, your down payment, your reserve cash, and the amount the bank will loan you. You can determine what a bank will loan you by getting pre-approved. If you will have to put five percent down and the bank will loan you up to $175,000, then you can look only at homes that are $175,000 or less — as long as you have the $8,750 for the down payment and at least one month's rent.

The hard part is determining whether the property you are looking at is a good buy.

A good rule of thumb is to look for a house at or below the median price range of a neighborhood. The median price range means that half the houses sold are more expensive and half are less expensive than the property you are considering. You can find the median home price by asking any real estate agent in your area. Median sale prices differ widely from region to region, and even from neighborhood to neighborhood.

By choosing homes that are at or below the median price, you are providing a more affordable home to your tenant while putting out less investment money to purchase the property.

Smaller houses also have higher returns, because you can get a higher rate per square foot than for larger homes. For instance, if you have a 1,000 square foot home and can rent it for $1,000, you are receiving $1 per square foot. On the other hand, if you have a 2,000 square foot home and can rent it for $1,500, you are only getting $0.75 per foot.

Do Not Judge a Book By Its Cover

You should not judge a home by its outside appearance. A home may look good and be in poor physical condition. Conversely, a home may look like it is in horrendous shape and only need some tender-loving care.

The best way to determine the real physical condition of a property is to have it inspected by a professional. The physical condition that you are willing to accept will be determined by your investment objectives. Some people want to only make minor repairs, while others look for homes that are in distress.

INVESTOR INSIGHT:

Ask to attend the walkthrough with the inspector. Watching how he inspects and what he looks for will give you tips on how to do your own preliminary inspections in the future.

Initially, you should look for homes that need few repairs. These homes will bring you the most profit because you will not need to spend much time on repairs before bringing in a rent check. You will also be able to maximize your ROI because your investment will be low compared to the money you will receive.

Even if you are willing to make repairs, you should avoid homes that have:

- Weak or bad foundations (large cracks in the drywall, larger than normal separations in brick mortar, and doorjambs and window casings out of alignment)
- Moisture problems (mold, which can get expensive)
- Old plumbing
- Out-of-date electrical wiring

Today or Tomorrow?

It is always the right time to buy.

If you know what you want out of a rental property, have your finances in order, have a network in place, and have done your research, you are ready to begin. It is possible to research and analyze yourself into inactivity and never get started.

There is no perfect deal — there are only good deals.

Been There, Done That

Renting out a home while also trying to sell it seems like a win-win situation — you generate income while also potentially closing on a sale. However, Michael Kelczewski, a Realtor with Brandywine Fine Properties SIR, explains that it isn't always as great as it sounds.

He had a property that was a challenge to market — it had a strange layout and an irregular proximity to the main road. He and the owner decided to lease the property while continuing the marketing period. He recalls, "The tenant persistently denied entrance to showing agents while leaving a giant, plastic cockroach tied to the stairwell! The individual would also close all the blinds to the point of near darkness before agents toured the home — many can attest to the alluring aspect that natural light can provide to a home. Needless to say, the lease was terminated after six months."

Can You Make It Work?

Knowing how much you can charge for rent is one of the keys to making a property work. Without being able to charge enough, you will not break even.

Finding the going rate for rental properties in your area is a simple task. There are plenty of real estate websites that provide information on rental units. Trulia, accessible at **www.trulia.com**, for example, allows you to search for rental availabilities in your neighborhood (or any neighborhood) and see how much in monthly rent the owners are seeking. Other websites that offer similar information include **www.homes.com**, **www.rentals.com** and **www.zillow.com**. You might also check the classified section of your local newspaper's website.

Most sites will allow you to search by the number of bedrooms and baths and other amenities. If the advertisement does not list a price, call and ask. Knowing what other landlords are charging for similar properties is essential to your business as it will help you establish what prospective tenants will pay for your property.

Just because you are renting a three-bedroom, two-bath house does not mean that it will bring in the same rent as another in your area. You have to look at the property as a whole and ask yourself these questions:

1. Does my property offer things to the tenant that other properties do not?
2. Is my property closer to shopping centers or main arteries?
3. Is my property in a better school district?
4. Is my property in a better neighborhood?

Honestly answering these questions will help you establish a rental rate, and then you can determine whether that rate will make you break even. If the answer is no, then the deal is not a good one.

Now that you know the criteria for finding the right rental home, you need to begin the hunt. In Chapter 4, we will explore the ins and outs of finding the right property.

CASE STUDY: JANE, INVESTOR AND LANDLORD

Jane is a small investor in Florida. She watched her parents invest in real estate throughout her childhood and learned much from them. First and foremost, she learned that knowing your market is essential.

"I was aware of the market. I think of real estate as my hobby. I love watching the market. My parents always told me to find something you like to do and then find a way to make money with it. Whenever I see a sign for sale in my neighborhood, or close by, I will call up. I do not have any intention of purchasing. I simply want to know what they are asking. You see, you listen, you read articles on real estate, and you keep yourself appraised on the market."

Jane got the itch and nearly bought a condo, but a trusted lender whom she had built a relationship with helped her see that it was not a good investment. "Thanks to him, I did not make a bad mistake. A good lender is important to have on your side."

She abandoned the deal on the property, but became disheartened and was not actively looking until a year later. She found something in the city, though she lived in a more rural area. She found a good property but was apprehensive.

"The gut feeling goes a long way. I was not comfortable. I was happy, but something just did not feel right. Certain factors were not right for us as buyers. My parents always warned me that buying a home far away can be difficult. There were many hassles unless you wanted to use a management company, and I knew that I wanted to do the landlording myself.

"How would I start renting the place? I would have to show up an hour away just to show it. The property made good sense in terms of money, but it was not without much time and effort. I convinced my husband that we had to cancel it. He was disappointed."

For Jane, finding areas that are similar to her own neighborhood makes determining whether a property is a good one much easier. Since she is more like her eventual tenants, she can answer questions about how her tenant would feel about living there and whether the house is close enough to the amenities her tenant will want.

To find properties in her area, Jane looks in many different locations, such as:

- **Realtor.com**
- Local newspaper
- Flyers
- **Craigslist.org**
- Websites providing MLS listings
- Bulletin announcements at the grocery store, bank, or other local area

She also watches every "for sale" sign in her neighborhood and will check each one out. Her research paid off after turning down the property in the city.

"We already had a locked in rate, so I started looking at everything in our local market. Because I had already done all the research in my own area, I was able to have a contract submitted for a house five minutes from my own in one week. I realized that going just a few miles too far beyond my area of expertise could make a possible good deal a bad one."

Jane believes that as long as you have done your research and know your market, there is never a bad time to buy. Timing is about finding the right bargain, not about market dips or time of the year. These issues may affect when you sell, but should not enter the equation when you buy. If you are financially able, the time is right.

Jane, though an absentee landlord, is a hands-on landlord. She and her husband find their own tenants, deal with tenant issues, maintain the property, and keep their own records. Larger projects will be contracted out to those who have more expertise.

In addition to having a good lender and a good contractor, Jane believes that having a good attorney is crucial. "I found a good attorney in Miami and I miss her so much because I do not have one at the moment. I talked with my realtor who recommended a good attorney. I used them once, and I like the company, but I did not click. Finding someone whom you click with and who can be the muscle standing behind you on a deal is a great feeling."

Each landlord has a different set of standards when finding a good tenant. For Jane, her tenants must have an excellent credit history for the past two years and good references from their last landlord. To her, the key to successful investing, after you find the right property, is finding good tenants.

"I was looking at a website, and it gave some good advice. As the potential renter pulls up, notice the condition of their car. How they keep their car is going to be similar to how they are going to treat your property. The article also suggested that you notice whether they wipe their feet before entering the house. I do this as I interview possible tenants. It eliminates many right away."

What will Jane do if she gets a bad tenant? "Find a good attorney — fast." She says you need to know the eviction process inside and out before you need it.

Jane did not realize how good it was to invest in property until she did it for herself. "Even if I have to pay some of the mortgage now and again, it certainly will not be more than a car payment. When I realized that, I said, 'Wow! I am getting so much more for the same amount of money.' If only people understood that."

Chapter 4

Ready or Not, Here I Come

*N*ow that you are ready to buy your first rental property, let us discuss where you should look. In this chapter, we will explore several avenues to find the right rental home: the internet, newspapers, magazines, local real estate agents, scouts, people who are selling by owner, and networks of real estate professionals.

Getting Web Savvy

Over the last few years, the number of real estate sites that cater to home-buyers has exploded. Some sites are national in scope. Others are hyper local. In any case, there is a vast array of resources available. The hard part may be zeroing in on the sites that are most appropriate given your goals.

Just about everyone these days starts their search with a few internet queries. You can simply do an online search with the words "homes for sale Raleigh, NC," for example. You will have a large list of sites to choose from. These sites can either be specialized sites that list properties from many areas or more local sites, often run by a specific agent.

The top real estate websites continue to roll out easy-to-use features that can greatly aid in your search. You can search according to myriad criteria, seek out comparable sales data, view properties in specific school districts, check out only homes within specific price ranges, view homes with a certain number of bedrooms or other criteria, take virtual tours, and so on. Many sites will also give you automatic updates and alerts when homes that meet your criteria are added to their database.

One very well-known site for this kind of search is hosted by the National Association of Realtors at **www.realtor.com**. Other sites include www.zillow.com, www.trulia.com, and www.redfin.com. Some sites, notably www.realtor.com and www.redfin.com, are linked to the Multiple Listing Service. These sites are updated often, some every 15 minutes, which is ideal in super-competitive markets.

Many real estate agencies and even specific agents offer websites that are very local in nature.

Given the rise of the local economy, you will not be surprised to learn that many of these sites also offer apps optimized for smartphones and other hand-held devices. In many cases, these apps offer just as much information as their companion websites.

✍ *Been There, Done That* ✍

Dawn Cook, the home stager and real estate investor in Indiana, uses a variety of methods to locate her investment properties. She explains:

"I found most of them FSBO. I feel the best ways to find rental properties are keeping a sharp eye out for good deals by checking the local MLS website often, watching for FSBOs, and asking questions of people whenever they mention a property for sale or about to go on sale. This keeps you informed and up to date on potential properties in an area that you may want to purchase a rental property. I avoid the paper, because today, things get sold quickly, and I do not feel that the paper gives enough information like the internet or a drive by of a FSBO."

Read All About It

One of the easiest ways to find a home for sale is by checking the classified section of your local newspaper, which just might be available online.

Ads in the newspaper can be created by real estate agents or For Sale By Owners (FSBOs). It does not matter who put the ad in the paper. What matters is whether the home for sale meets your criteria.

One way to find a good property is to look for certain words in the advertisements. Some phrases to watch out for might be:

- Investment opportunity
- Great rental property
- Seller is motivated
- Seller is flexible
- Starter home

For example:

FSBO, **LAKE TILLERY**, A-Frame 3BR fixer-upper, annual views Moro Mtn and Lake, $147,000

Or

Reduced! Home for Sale! Renovated 2BR/1BA, ½ ac with detached garage. New kitchen and floors. Covered front porch, Large back deck. Fenced back yard.

Or

MOTIVATED SELLER 2,700 sq ft brick house in Robbins. 4 or 5BR/1BA, basement, hardwood floors, **Needs some TLC. Priced below tax value.** $91,000.

Homes that meet these descriptions are often in older, more established neighborhoods. These neighborhoods are a good place to find a rental home.

Call the number and look at the home. Even if you decide that the home is not for you, you will have a new contact with the advertiser, who is hopefully a real estate agent. Talk with them about what you need. They may be able to help you or put you in contact with a realtor in their office who specializes in investment properties.

❧ Been There, Done That ❧

Debbie Malone bought a four family unit for $30,000 five years ago that was a HUD foreclosure. It was not listed correctly. Instead of showing the property as a multi-tenant unit, it showed it as a two-bedroom single-family dwelling. In actuality, it had two units with two bedrooms, an efficiency unit, and an unfinished unit. Even with the three units rented, it was a cash cow. Debbie said, "We would say 'moo' every time we drove by. We sold it two years ago for $92,000."

Another way to use the classified section of the paper is to place your own ad in the "real estate wanted" section. This type of advertising does not need to be costly. All you are trying to do is let people know exactly what you are looking for.

Your ad needs to be specific. If you only want three or four bedroom homes with two or more baths, be sure to say so. You should not waste your time on homes that do not meet this criterion.

For example:

Seeking apartment buildings to purchase. Wanting 120 to 150 units. Must be within ten miles of downtown. Call 1-555-555-1234

Or you can be more specific:

Looking for single family home or town home
in the $500,000 to $650,000 range.
Minimum 3 bedrooms and 2 baths.
Square footage between 1,500 and
2,100 square feet
Home not older than 20 years
In excellent school district
In the following areas: San Jose, Cupertino,
Sunnyvale, Santa Clara
Call 1-555-555-1234

Real Estate Magazines

Other good sources of homes are the local real estate magazines. Almost every area publishes a magazine, either weekly or monthly, that shows homes for sale. Some areas have more than one magazine. You can find these magazines outside real estate offices, drug stores, grocery stores, and local gathering places.

Real estate agents or a group of agents put out these magazines. They list all of their houses on one or two pages, give you their contact information, and tell you why you should purchase your home from them. This information may give you some insight into the type of realtor who has the property for sale.

If you see a home that interests you, call the agent. Although most agents in these publications deal with traditional retail housing, you may get lucky and find an agent who specializes in investment properties. Even if they do not, they may have a property that will suit your needs.

INVESTOR INSIGHT:

Real estate magazines can be a good source of real estate related products and services. Such services include real estate agents, mortgage companies, appraisers, surveyors, title companies, real estate attorneys, and insurance companies.

Ask a Pro

Talking with someone in the business is a good idea. The type of agent you are looking for is someone who:

- Works full-time
- Is internet savvy
- Loves their job
- Uses new technologies
- Has handled investment properties in the past

Your chosen agent should be in the day-to-day loop of his business so that he can bring you new properties as they become available. A good agent will always be on the lookout for a good deal on a property that meets your specifications. You will have to share with them exactly what you are looking for; otherwise, they will bring you deals that will waste your time and theirs.

Real estate agents, by law, have to act in your best interest. They are required to do everything possible to help you find a good deal and make sound investment decisions. They can provide you with up-to-date market information, such as comparable sales data, to make your decisions more accurate.

There is no need to be limited to one real estate agent. Realtor A may be well-known among some circles, and Realtor B among others. Although there may be some overlap, each will have sources unknown to the other. Having a broader reach is beneficial to your investment goals.

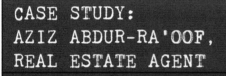

CASE STUDY: AZIZ ABDUR-RA'OOF, REAL ESTATE AGENT

Columbia, MD
RE/MAX Rewards –
RE/MAX International Inc.
Office (301) 474-1515
Mobile (240) 994-9553

Aziz is a realtor in Maryland, but he does not limit his investment purchases to those he finds on his own. "A realtor mentioned something to me and I started looking at the area and did much research on my own. The home was a FSBO. I talked with the owners and decided it was a good deal. Why didn't the realtor who gave me the lead take the deal? I assume that the house did not meet his investing criteria, nor did it meet the criteria of his real estate business. For me, opportunity and favorable terms make a good deal."

Aziz also looks at foreclosures as a source of investment properties, but he cautions that this may be something to avoid if you do not know foreclosure law or have a trusted attorney who does.

On the note of foreclosures, and property owners in distress, Aziz gives a caution to investors. "We are in the people business. If someone does not want their home anymore or cannot afford to stay in their home anymore, this will make a good deal for you. However, it is imperative that you do not take advantage of them. The Golden Rule applies: Do not do something to someone that you would not want done to you."

One of Aziz's best experiences with a purchase came about with an owner who simply needed to get out of his home. "When I spoke directly to the owner, he threw out a number. The number seemed high to me, so I used a technique that I learned. I asked him what amount he would be willing to sell his home for in cash in seven days, and then I shut up. There will be silence. Wait until they start to speak. He wanted out with a quick sale. I wanted the house. I believe in a win-win. In his case, it was not as much about price as it was about timing. He wanted to move on with his life and a quick closing met that need. I ended up getting the house for less than his original number, but it was a fair price for him."

For Aziz, determining whether a property is right is as simple as running the analysis. If it meets your criteria and the numbers make sense, then the property is right for you.

For instance, if you focus on homes that are in the entry-level phase, you will see those that pop up that meet this criterion. Since you have already researched the area, you know whether it is a good price, and you know the rental prices in the area. You can look at the school system and other amenities like proximity to jobs or big cities.

When Aziz decides on a home, he looks closely at the physical shape of the home. If problems are merely cosmetic, he does not worry too much. Larger issues, like plumbing, take more consideration as he determines whether it will fit into his budget and the acquisition price.

"If I think I can get it done in a reasonable amount of time and with a reasonable amount of money, I will do it. I look at it as a way to get at a lower price. The caveat is that I am sure I have the people to come in to do the repairs immediately."

Aziz advises that you put together a team, though he suggests that it can happen over time. "I like talking to other realtors who are investors and other investors. I am always looking to see if there is someone out there who can help me, like a painter, an insurance agent, or a carpet layer. I am always networking."

Although he is capable of a few minor repairs, Aziz feels that it is in his best financial interest to get a professional to do the work for him. He assesses what needs to be fixed and then hires out. He says that it is important to watch for trends. For instance, carpet is no longer "in," so he often replaces worn carpet with hardwood floors.

The more you buy and fix up, the easier it becomes. "Once you fix one up, you have a template in your mind and do the same thing to all the properties. Tubs, paint, and carpet are the same for each similar unit. It allows me to get the house ready for rent as quickly as possible. I just stay out of the way and let others do their work."

Finally, Aziz has a word about leases — use one. "A lease is necessary, because we forget. We can make a minor mistake that can turn out to be a major issue. If you have everything written down, you and your tenants can reference back to it. Not using a lease is setting yourself up for failure."

For Aziz, real estate is a good investment whether the market is up or down. It is not a get rich quick scheme, but if you stick to your plan, you can realize your investment goals.

Scout It Out

A scout is someone who can find a house for you that meets your investment criteria. Anyone can be a scout. All it takes is an understanding of what you are looking for and the ability to provide you with leads with the appropriate information.

Such information includes:

- Location of the home
- Condition of the home
- Condition of the neighborhood

- Asking price
- Seller's terms
- Any timing requirements
- Degree of urgency
- Comparable sales data

A good scout will always be looking out for houses that meet your needs. They then pass this information on to you so you can make a final decision. If you purchase the home, then your scout will get monetary compensation known as a finder's fee. Finder's fees are often in the neighborhood of $500, but are only paid when the information leads to an actual purchase of a property.

Using a scout will broaden the scope of your search and help you find the best deals.

FSBOs

Another way to find a home is by looking to those selling their own homes. These sellers are known as FSBOs. Their goal is to save money by selling their property without a real estate agent.

There are plenty of websites that list properties up for sale by owner (FSBO). These include **www.forsalebyowner.com**, **www.fsbo.com**, **www. homesbyowner.com**, **www.byowner.com** and **www.zillow.com/for-sale-by-owner**.

Those selling their home often place a FSBO sign in the front yard or have listed their property in the paper. Checking out these signs and ads is a good way to find properties that may go unseen by agents or real estate magazines. If not caught at the right time, you can even miss an FSBO home in the paper.

INVESTOR INSIGHT:

Most FSBO sellers turn to a realtor within 60 to 90 days of putting their home on the market. You may be able to get a good deal during this time period, as they are more likely to give you the discount rather than pay a realtor's fee.

Networking

Getting your name out in your community as a real estate investor will help you find properties, and affiliating with a professional organization is a good way to do just that. Professional organizations include local groups, such as the chamber of commerce, or a local real estate investor's club. It can also mean a regional or national organization, such as the National Association of Home Builders.

INVESTOR INSIGHT:

Joining at least two clubs will help you gain the type of network needed to be successful in real estate investing.

You can find investment clubs near you by going to either **www. reiclub.com/real-estate-clubs.php** or **www.creonline.com/Real-Estate-Investment-Clubs/index.html**. You can also find these associations by looking in the yellow pages or by doing an internet search.

✑ Been There, Done That ✑

Marilynn Currie of Canada tells this story of a friendship that spawned an investment empire.

"My dentist is the millionaire next door. Unassuming and friendly, he lives in the family home that he bought when his children were small. He drives a small car that gets him from home to work and, on good days, he bicycles.

"As he said to me while working on my teeth, 'My wife says I have the same underwear that I wore in graduate school.'

"Way back in the late '70s, he had as a patient a young Realtor who needed major dental work. And as he was a young man growing his practice, they struck up a great friendship. Thereafter, the Realtor would schedule his appointments just before the lunch hour and then with the two-hour window of time, they were off looking at investment properties.

With a little bit of financial wizardry, he often bought two homes a week.

"Now, thirty or so years later, his investment properties are all over the world, from Canada to China to the U.S.A. — 55 homes and counting. He recently bought a defunct ice cream plant and sells his major output to Costco. Three of his children are now in dental school in Philadelphia, so he bought two town houses and his kids rent the rooms out to fellow students. He says when tuition is due, 'If there is not enough scholarship money, I just sell one of my homes, and pay the tuition.'

"I asked him what his secret was of such success. He said, 'Choose a Realtor you can trust, have a great banker, make sure your rent for the properties pays all the costs plus repairs, and choose your tenants carefully.'

"And who runs the business? His wife, of course. They keep it all in the family."

Using the methods found in this chapter, you will be able to find properties that will make a good start on your investment portfolio. In the next chapter, we will explore methods of determining whether the property makes monetary sense.

Chapter 5

Will the Property Make Money?

ash flow is essential, so checking the numbers is imperative. The property must show that it will make money.

To keep from paying too much, you need to determine the value of the property. If you have a car or a rare coin, you can look in a book to determine its value. The problem is that there is no book to look in to determine the value of real estate.

It is essential that you learn to estimate the value for yourself. This process is not difficult, especially since you can find much of the needed information on the internet.

Market value is the most likely price a property could bring in a competitive market. Do not confuse a home's market value with its tax-assessed value.

The tax-assessed value is determined when someone in the tax department of your city or county looks at the property and determines a value. Depending on your area, a tax assessment can be as little as 70 percent of the fair market value. The appraised value is determined by a licensed appraiser and is based on the price of similar homes in the area.

There are three main methods used by real estate investors to determine the value of their property. The rest of this chapter will be devoted to these methods.

Comparative Market Analysis

This method is the one most used to determine whether the price you are paying is the right price.

INVESTOR INSIGHT:

For a rental property, you will need to know whether you will make money based on the rent. Therefore, a Comparative Market Analysis (CMA) is a good place to start.

A CMA bases a property value on surrounding properties that have recently sold. These properties are similar in size, amenities, and features. To be accurate, the comps must be based on properties that were not sold at low prices or using financing not available to the average buyer.

A good CMA will address the following items:

Location: You should first look at properties that are in the same neighborhood as the one you plan to buy. Differences in location can be difficult to adjust for. Do not use comp houses that are outside the school district or in another town.

Time: Use comp data that is no more than six months old. If it is a slow market, you may have to go back further. Also, use only closed sales. The price could change on pending sales.

Housing Style: Look at houses that are the same style as the one you are looking at. Also, look at the zoning of the area. Do not compare houses that are in different zoning, such as a residential to a commercial.

Size: Be sure your comp has a similar house and lot size.

Rooms: Try to find homes that are similar in the number of bedrooms and baths. Also, find homes that have the same kind of family room, garage, utilities, or basement.

Condition: Condition is best assessed by a drive-by and can only be accounted for by looking on the outside. You can supplement what you see by the data on the MLS. Look for things like maintenance free exteriors, flooring, new kitchens and baths, and other improvements.

Age: It is best to compare homes that are of a similar age. If the only homes available for comps are far different, you will have to adjust.

INVESTOR INSIGHT:

Using the figure of $1,000 per year difference is a good way to adjust for age. If a comp home is 20 years old and your home is only eight years old, you can add $12,000 to the value of your home.

You can get the information you need from any area real estate agent. Most agents can even send the comps to you online.

Income Method

When you have determined whether you can buy the property at a good price, then it is time to see whether the property will make you any money. You will need to learn about Capitalization Rates and Gross Rent Multipliers.

The Capitalization Rate (cap rate) is determined by dividing the property's net operating income by its purchase price. The income you make will have to pay for the mortgage, insurance, taxes, and repairs. A cap rate below eight percent will erase your profits and begin to cost you money.

For instance, if you find a piece of property for $150,000 and it generates $1,000 per month, the cap rate would be eight percent. (Net income is $1,000 times 12 months, so the cap rate is $12,000 divided by $150,000.)

If you had to pay $175,000 for the same piece of property, your cap rate would be seven percent — too low to be considered a good deal.

The Gross Rent Multiplier (GRM) is the sales price divided by the monthly gross income of the property. In the case of the $150,000 property above, the GRM would be 150. Now, take the Gross Rent Multiplier of 150 and multiply it by the gross yearly rent of $12,000 to get a figure of $180,000. According to the GRM method, the home is worth $30,000 more than you are paying for it.

Of course, you are assuming that $1,000 is the right rent to charge and that it will pay the bills and provide you with a profit. Let us see if $1,000 will do that.

1. Mortgage Payment	$_____
2. Insurance Payment	$_____
3. Monthly Taxes	$_____
4. Monthly Maintenance	$_____
5. Monthly Repairs	$_____
6. Monthly Utility	$_____
7. Monthly Admin Cost	$_____
8. Other Monthly Debt	$_____
9. Monthly Vacancy Reserve	$_____
10. Monthly ROI	$_____
Total Expenses (Add Lines 1 thru 10)	$_____
Rental Price per Unit (Line 11 divided by # of units)	$_____

First, you will want to know the mortgage payment, your insurance, and your property taxes. This information can be obtained from your loan officer.

For the next several categories, you will need information from the owner. If they used the property as a rental before, you will want their Schedule E, their income and expense statement, and all the rental agreements from the past year. Additionally, you will want utility bills and repair and capital improvement bills from the last year. If the property has never been rented in the past, you will only be able to get the utility and capital improvement bills.

After you have collected this information from the owner, you will want to determine the monthly maintenance expense. This includes things like trash removal, yard work, snow removal, and minor repairs. If you have a figure for the year, divide it by 12 to get the monthly amount.

Next, you need to figure the repairs amount. This is money you will need to set aside for larger repairs such as the roof or the heating unit. You will need to look at the average life expectancy of:

- Roof
- Electrical system
- Plumbing
- HVAC unit
- Appliances
- Exterior paint
- Vinyl siding

Determine how many of these items you will need to replace over the next five years and add up the price of the replacement. Divide by 60 (five years is 60 months) to get the monthly amount you should have in reserve.

Next, you need to find out utility costs for a year and then divide by 12 to get a monthly cost. If you will not be paying the utilities for the property, simply put a zero in this category.

Administrative costs can be found by looking at the owner's Schedule E and income/expense statement. These are such things as advertising, accounting and legal services, office supplies, and even gas used to go to and from the property.

If you plan to do a rehab or other large improvement, figure the total and divide by 12 to find "other" debt.

You will then want to set aside a vacancy reserve. This is money needed to pay the mortgage when the unit is vacant. Most investors suggest having one percent. Divide this amount by 12 to get the monthly reserve.

Finally, to determine the ROI you are seeking, you should seek out the counsel of your accountant. A five to eight percent return would be considered good. When this number is determined, divide it by 12 to provide your monthly investment return.

Now, add up all those numbers to find your total monthly expenses. Divide that number by the number of units and you will have the average rental per unit.

Let us get back to our example. The property you wish to buy is $150,000 for a single-family home. You will put down $30,000 so your mortgage will be for $120,000 at 6.11 percent for 30 years. You also want an eight percent ROI on your investment. The other figures were obtained from the owner of the property and the need for about $3,000 in repairs over the next five years.

1. Mortgage Payment $727
2. Insurance Payment $100

3. Monthly Taxes	$75
4. Monthly Maintenance	$50
5. Monthly Repairs	$50
6. Monthly Utility	$0
7. Monthly Admin Cost	$20
8. Other Monthly Debt	$0
9. Monthly Vacancy Reserve	$125
10. Monthly ROI	$200
Total Expenses	$1,347
(Add Lines 1 thru 10)	
Rental Price per Unit	$1,347
(Line 11 divided by # of units)	

To pay the bills and earn your desired ROI, you will have to charge $1,350 per month in rent. Whether that amount is a good deal depends on the area. If the homes in the area that are like yours rent for about the same, the number works. If, on the other hand, the properties rent for $1,000, you are not likely to find a renter for your unit at $1,350. Even if you wanted a zero ROI, you will be losing $150 a month by offering the home at $1,000 per month.

❦ Been There, Done That ❦

Chris Lengquist has this to say about determining whether a property is a good investment:

"The first property I bought, I forgot to figure in the Homeowner's Association fees and a reasonable vacancy and repair fund. That is not the fault of real estate investing. That is the fault of someone not knowing what he is doing. Most of my bad stories start and stop with something that should have been under my control."

Replacement Cost Method

This method estimates how much it would cost you to replace the structures on the property without the cost of the land. These costs are determined

by dividing the total number of square feet in a building by the per square foot construction cost of a new building.

For example, a 2,000 square foot home in an area where $175/square foot is typical for new construction would cost $350,000. Therefore, if the home was selling for less than $350,000, the replacement cost method would suggest that it is a good deal.

You can find out the replacement cost by calling an insurance broker. In the case of our $150,000 home, using the replacement cost of $110/square foot on the 1,500 square foot home would give us a value of $165,000, suggesting that this would be a good deal.

Different methods tell you different things. The comp model and replacement model deal strictly with the cost of the property. In both, the property is a good deal. When looking at the income related models, the CAP rate looks good, but the GRM shows that the property cannot sustain itself based on the rents in the neighborhood.

As someone merely wishing to buy a home for his or her own, this house represents a good deal. But as an investor, you would want to pass it by.

CASE STUDY: STEVE ALEFF

Steve Aleff
(218) 728-0488

For Steve Aleff, an investor in Duluth, Minnesota, it is easy to know whether a property is a good one. He explains, "I look at the bedroom number and quality based on the price of the property. I allow $300 per bedroom in rent multiplied by the number of bedrooms at 80 percent times 100. That will give you the most you can afford to pay for a property and have positive net cash flow with a 20 percent down payment on the purchase. For example, a six bedroom house at $300/bedroom = $1,800. $1,800 x 80 percent = $1,440. Multiply this by 100 and you get $144,000. That is the maximum price I would be willing to spend on this property."

This formula will not work for everyone in all areas because rents differ so much. Instead, you might want to simply put in the figure for the rent and then do the rest of the math.

For Steven, pristine is not a condition of purchase. "All of the properties I acquired had a story or issue. We look for situations that will put us in a position to acquire the properties at values that fit our model. These situations include death, estate, relocation, job change, moving to assisted living, empty nesters, or bankruptcy. We rely on involvement in the community both by us and our realtor who understands completely our model so as not to waste time with properties outside the parameters.

"Some people say we should be more diverse, but we are happy with college rental houses because our tenants will always be there as long as the college is. We have no issues with migration or population changes. All of our properties now are within three blocks of a college and are highly desirable for the tenants we market to.

"That is why real estate is a good marketing choice for me, even in a soft market. When I do my homework and believe it is a good investment given current rental prices, then I am going to go ahead with the deal.

"People who use a firm strategy in purchasing will always find opportunities to take advantage of market forces and pricing. Value investing is critical. If tenants are adequate and vacancies are limited, this investment allows for margin to be used in a way that will lend itself to mandatory repayment and positive net cash flow — unlike many strategies in the market system."

Finding good tenants is also a part of Steve's plan. He knows how important it is to market and brand your company name in the community. People want to rent from a reputable landlord. Creating a logo and quality brochures and flyers will give prospective tenants a good impression.

What is the best advice that Steve can give to anyone going into rental property investing?

"Treat your current tenants like gold. They are paying off your margin and giving you positive cash flow. They talk, so make sure they say good things about you."

Investor Insights

When purchasing a home for investment purposes, you need to look at the numbers and trust your instincts. Here are a few things you can do to make the process easier:

1. Compare, compare, compare. When you think you have found the right property, inspect it again. Compare it to others you have seen and determine whether it has the features that are important to you.

2. Know the property values in the area, the growth rate, the expected growth rate, the expected income of the property, and any other information that will help you decide whether the area is good for you.

3. Do not spend much time at a property until you have crunched the numbers. You do not want to get emotionally attached to a property that makes no financial sense.

4. Do not go it alone. Ask other investors for their opinions. Ask questions and get answers from real estate agents, loan officers, and others in the business.

5. Know what you want before you get started. Determine how many investment properties you want to buy, the approximate ROI you expect from these properties, the debt level you are comfortable with, the area of town you wish to purchase in, and other similar items. Knowing what you want will keep you from wasting your time looking at homes that do not meet your needs.

6. Land will always appreciate in value. Buildings can be maintained but do not appreciate. Therefore, make sure that the value of the land is 30 percent or more of the price of the property.

7. Lowball your offers. The lower you can buy a home for below market value, the more you will make on it now and in the future. Even if the low offer is rejected, keep it on the table. They may decide to come back to it if the home stays on the market too long.

8. Get known. When more people know you as an investment buyer, more deals will come your way. You should get to know CPAs, lawyers, real estate agents, loan officers, and anyone else who knows about real estate investing.

❦ *Been There, Done That* ❧

Dawn Cook loves to talk of a deal that made sense no matter which way you measure it:

"We bought a commercial building that had a one bedroom apartment above it with space below for commercial use. We used the space below for our own business for a while and used the rent from the apartment above to offset our overhead. Then, we rented the lower space out and the rent for that space covered our mortgage payment so the upper unit was pure profit. We later flipped it and made a nice profit."

When you have an investment property that meets your specifications, it is time to purchase it. The loan process for real estate investments is a bit different from that of a homeowner. In Chapter 6, we will review the different types of loans available to investors.

Pot of Gold

You have found the perfect property, and now you want the perfect loan. The truth is that finding a loan for an investment property is more difficult than finding one for a residence. You will be asked to make a larger down payment, accept a higher interest rate, carry a higher credit rating, and meet more financial requirements. In short, you will be held to a higher standard at every turn.

But fear not. Loans for investment properties are available; you just need to know how and where to find them. In the end, you just might end up with a loan from a non-traditional lender.

Where to Start?

The name of the game these days is the internet. Just as homebuyers should start their search by tapping free online resources, so should mortgage seekers begin by launching a browser. You will have plenty of options for mortgage loans these days, as a quick internet search will make clear. Just about all lenders — traditional banks and credit unions, online-only upstarts and mortgage brokers — have active programs to allow people to seek mortgages online. Making sense of all the choices can be difficult.

To be sure, the online trend can make things easier for mortgage hunters. In some cases, you can search for ideal loan terms, apply for loans, and monitor the approval process all with a few clicks or finger taps. No matter what, when going through the process, you will be better off if you arm yourself with basic knowledge. Convenience in some cases can lead to misinformation for consumers who are unfamiliar with the process. For example, some lenders will provide quick interest rate quotes online that are not meant to be actual annual percentage rates, which factor in fees and expenses. The difference can be significant.

At some point, if you want a real quote from a lender, you must be prepared to input critical information about your annual income, your debt obligations, credit scores, tax information, the amount you are seeking, and so forth.

Be aware also that the extent of online services will differ considerably from lender to lender. Some will offer highly automated online processes that allow you to complete virtually the entire process. That includes such tasks as gathering bank statements and the like. Others firms will require you to go offline to complete the process.

In any case, while the online marketplace may seem confusing, you would be wise to explore your many online options. The more options you consider, the more likely you will be to lock in a loan with the most favorable terms. And that can make all the difference between a good deal and a great deal for budding real estate investors.

Surprisingly, a report from the Consumer Financial Protection Bureau found that less than half of prospective homebuyers actually shop for the best deals. You should strive to avoid that potentially costly mistake. At a minimum, you should seek specific mortgage information from two or three lenders.

Mortgage Providers in the Digital Age

There are three main types of mortgage providers these days:

- **Traditional banks and credit unions.** They are increasingly moving their operations online, offering more convenience to customers. It wouldn't hurt to check out the offerings from your bank or credit union, especially if you have a longstanding relationship with the institution.

- **Online mortgage companies.** These are companies that make loans and operate according to online business models. Examples include Social Finance (SoFi) and Quicken Loans. In many cases, most of your dealings with the firms will be online, which can make the process more efficient.

- **Mortgage marketplaces and brokers.** These entities strive to generate leads for multiple mortgage companies, aiming to earn a fee if a loan is actually issued. Examples of such marketplaces include Zillow, E-Loan and LendingTree. Many mortgage brokers have also moved online. These brokers also work with multiple lending institutions and aim to guide you to one of them.

While the real estate market has been booming, mortgage lenders are in some ways as picky as ever. The housing crisis of 2008 changed the mortgage industry in profound ways, leading to a slew of new regulations and tightened lending standards.

That said, as the real estate market remains strong in most areas of the country, mortgage lenders are actively competing for the most qualified borrowers. Hopefully, that includes you. If you have a strong income, a great credit score, low debt, and lots of cash on hand, you will likely be pleasantly surprised by how eager lenders will be to work with you. In some high-income areas, such as Silicon Valley, lenders are offering highly bespoke loans, 24-hour approval processes, and related financial planning services to entice people. Some are lending enough to cover the entire cost of the property, not even requiring a down payment. Of course, people seeking loans for an investment property will be viewed differently.

Indeed, not everyone is in the enviable position of qualifying for these programs. Tobie Stanger, writer for Consumer Reports, notes several groups of people that might be denied the best interest rates in general:

- **The self-employed.** You must be able to demonstrate consistent, if not rising, income over several years, backed up by proper tax returns and other documentation.

- **People with low credit scores (FICO).** In general, you need a minimum FICO score of 760 to qualify for rock-bottom interest rates. Knowing your score is important. Fortunately, you are entitled a free report from each of three main credit-reporting agencies per year.

- **People with too much debt.** Mortgage lenders obviously will prefer applicants will little additional debt. Stanger writes that mortgage lenders in general prefer people whose mortgage payment will be roughly 28 percent of their monthly gross income. All debt — mortgage, credit cards, and so on — should be 36 percent or less.

- **People who can't afford a suitable down payment.** The more you can pay upfront, the better you will look in the eyes of mortgage lenders. One novel option is to consider ways to boost your down payment, perhaps by selling other assets, seeking assistance from family members, and even crowdfunding on such sites as **www.GoFundMe.com**.

What Rainbow to Seek Under

Not all real estate loans are the same. It will be up to you to choose a loan.

There are three main loan attributes that will affect the loan and your loan payments:

1. Interest rate
2. Amortization period
3. Loan amount

A change in any one of these three can make a substantial difference to whether a property will make money.

Interest rate

The interest rate is the amount of money you will be charged to borrow the funds. This amount is over and above the principal due. For instance, if you take out a loan for $150,000 at seven percent interest over 30 years, the total amount of interest you will pay over the life of the loan is $209,263.35. This amount is over and above the initial loan amount of $150,000.

Interest rates differ widely from month to month and from loan to loan, which is why you must look at many different loans to find the right fit for you.

When determining how much interest will affect you, you must look at the amount borrowed and over what time. Small loans, such as a loan for $100,000, will not be affected much by interest rates variations of 1 percent or less. But large loans, in the millions, will be affected considerably, even by ¼ of a percent over the period of the loan.

Amortization period

The amortization period is the length of time used to calculate loan payments. These payments are determined assuming the loan will be repaid over the stated period. An amortization table shows a list of payments made over the life of the loan and which part of the payment is going to interest and which part to principal.

When you have a short amortization period, your loan payments will be higher, but the overall interest you pay will be less, and the time it takes to acquire equity in the home will decrease. Conversely, a longer amortization period lowers your payment but increases the amount of interest paid and the time it takes to gain equity in the home.

Loan amount

The loan amount is the amount being borrowed. The more money you borrow, the higher your loan payment will be. Some believe that putting a large amount of money down on a property, and thus making the payments low, is the best way to create a rental investment loan. This is an unwise idea.

When investing, you want to leverage other people's money. By doing so, you follow the axiom:

> *The more money you borrow, the greater will be*
> *your return on your invested capital.*

By using the bank's money instead of your own, you will generate enough income to pay the loan and make a profit. The profit will be defined as a ratio based on the initial investment. Therefore, the ROI is greater when you have less of your own money invested.

Other factors to consider

You will also want to look at the down payment, term of the loan, the associated fees and any prepayment penalties.

Down payment: Many mortgage lenders will require a down payment of 20 percent of the loan amount as a strong sign of your commitment to the deal. For a primary residence mortgage, you find loans that require a much smaller down payment provided that you buy private mortgage insurance. However, when it comes to rental properties, mortgage insurance will not be accepted. You will be required to come up with a sizable down payment.

Term: The term of the loan is the life of the loan. You can have a five-year loan term amortized over a 30-year period, meaning that the payments will be based as if you will pay over a 30-year period, but the loan ends in just five years. At the end of the term, you will either have to repay the loan in full or renegotiate the loan.

Figuring out the best term for your loan depends on the plans you have for your investment. If you are planning to hold your investment for ten years or more, you will most likely want a loan with a term that matches the amortization period. If you took a shorter term, you would be forced to refinance when the term was up and perhaps end up with a bad rate.

Long-term property works best with long-term loans. If a better financing situation becomes available during your ownership of the property, you always have the option of refinancing the loan.

If you plan to keep the property for a year or two while you rent it and fix it up, then you might want to consider a much shorter loan term. Loans with shorter terms have lower rates, which would be to your advantage. For example, a three-year Adjustable Rate Mortgage (ARM) is ½ to 1 percent lower than a 30-year fixed mortgage.

Fees: Loan fees can be one of the biggest expenses to an investment property financial deal. Such fees include:

- Application fees: Loan application fees are paid at the time the application is made and can range up to $500, but not all lenders charge such a fee. The fee is used to pay for costs of the loan officer or broker going over the application and getting the documents together to help them determine whether they can lend you money.

- Underwriting fees: These fees are associated with the underwriter for processing the loan application.

- Loan origination fees (also known as origination points): These fees are equivalent to one point or one percent of the total loan amount. These fees pay for the legal documents that must be drawn up and the processing of these documents.

- Points: A point is equal to one percent of your loan amount, meaning that, if you pay two points for a loan of $100,000, you would pay an extra $2,000. Points are used to get you a lower interest rate. Each point you pay will most often lower your interest rate by ¼ of a percent. Almost every lender has discount point loan levels. They may offer options with no points, one point, two points, or even more. If you plan to keep your property for a long time, paying for points up front makes sense. If you plan to sell within five years, paying points will end up costing you money.

INVESTOR INSIGHT:

Some lenders advertise their interest with no points while others advertise their lowest possible rate that includes points. Be sure to compare apples to apples when comparison-shopping for loans.

Oh, the Paperwork

When you are ready to take out a loan, the lender will need a long list of documents, including:

- Loan application
- Purchase agreement
- Financial statement
- Income and balance statements for your business
- Income tax returns for at least the last two years
- Verification of cash required for down payment
- Credit references
- FICO report
- Property operating statements for property currently used as a rental unit
- Leases used for current rental property
- Property taxes for rental property
- Insurance binder for rental property

- Survey
- Appraisal

There are several ways to get financing for your property that do not require the traditional 20 to 40 percent down and/or the higher interest rates.

You can consider:

- Private Mortgage Lending
- Seller Financing
- Owner-Occupied Loans

Financing your investment property makes sense, as long as you do your homework and choose the right loan vehicle for your needs.

❧ *Been There, Done That* ☙

Aziz Abdur-Ra'oof learned this lesson the hard way:

"I bought a home and purchased it outright. It was not the right thing to do. I tied up too much money. I will try to put 10 to 20 percent down. I can do this by finding loans with private mortgage lenders. I prefer not to go through a bank due to all the excess fees and the amount of money I have to put down."

Private Mortgage Lending

Private mortgage lending, sometimes referred to as hard money lending, means that you borrow your money from an individual rather than a bank. The interest rates will be higher, but the speed and ease of the deal are excellent.

You can find people who wish to be private mortgage lenders in a variety of places because most people would love to see 10 to 12 percent return on their money with that investment secured by real estate. Anyone — from a member of your church to your neighbor — may be someone who can lend you money for your investment deal.

You can also approach a mortgage broker. They often have several clients who wish to invest their money this way.

A private mortgage loan does not exceed 75 percent of the loan-to-value ratio (the loan amount divided by the fair market price of the home). Let those who are potential lenders know this information and understand that the loans are done on a per property basis. In return, you will ask that they make a quick decision and can have the money to you in 10 days or less.

After your lender has approved the investment, the funds are sent to the closing attorney and held in escrow, which should make your lender feel better, too. You will never handle their money.

After the closing, your lender will receive a promissory note, a mortgage on the property, lenders' title insurance, and will be listed as the lender on the hazard insurance policy.

The process is a win-win for everyone. You only pay interest on the loan, you get no origination or discount fees, and you do not have to worry about lenders and their rules concerning investment properties. Your lender receives considerable interest and a secure investment.

It is a perfect situation if you can get the property below value.

Let us say that you can get a $100,000 property for $75,000 because it is in distress. But you have calculated that with $5,000, you can get the property up to par and then rent it out for $1,000 per month.

You find a private lender who is willing to pay the entire $75,000 at 10 percent on the property because it is only 75 percent LTV. You use $5,000 you would have spent toward a down payment to fix the property and get it rented. At the end of a year, you have paid $7,500 in interest fees and $5,000 in initial repairs while earning $12,000 in rent. This situation leaves you $500 out of pocket for the year, which is far less than a down payment of 30 percent on a loan of $75,000.

In year two, you make another $2,000 in repairs, pay another $7,500 in interest, and once again, make $12,000 in rent. This situation gives you a profit of $2,500. You do the same thing for three more years, making a total of $9,500 in profit, and then put the house up for sale. It sells for the market value of $100,000; you pay off your private lender and walk away with $25,000.

In just five years, you took $500 (your net expense at the end of year one) and turned it into nearly $35,000. You are happy and so is your lender who got their initial investment back plus $7,500 a year for five years.

You can repeat this process, even having several private loans for several different properties at once.

CASE STUDY: ETHAN DOZEMAN

Ethan Dozeman, GRI
Remax Grand Valley
(616) 292-7329
www.homes.com/real-estate-agents/
ethan-dozeman/id-19856287

Ethan Dozeman is a real estate agent, but he plans to be a real estate mogul before he is through. "I have seven properties now. My wife and I bought our first home in Grand Rapids. It was a starter house in a transitional neighborhood. We decided to move and rent it out. The renter has been there for four years. That got us started on our venture.

"My target goal is 30 by the age of 30. If I get four or five a year, I will have 30 by 30. That may be a bit aggressive, and I am willing to tone it down a bit. But I do not think there is a number of investment properties that is too many. You just have to remember that you will need to hire out more of the work and figure that into your numbers."

Ethan is realizing his dream by leveraging other people's money. Private mortgage investing has gotten him into several deals with no money down. He has also used traditional financing, but he knows that after he reaches 10 properties, he will have to get commercial loans.

"I like repossessions. I did one deal with a group of investors. They bought the house for $65,000 and signed me onto the deed. After they fixed it up, the appraised value was $106,000. I did a refinance on the property and got an 80 percent LTV, meaning I got a loan of $84,800, paid the investor back his $65,000 and another $24,000, and now have a home that is worth $106,000 with no money invested."

According to Ethan, real estate is a good investment because you have the advantage of leverage. You can go to the bank and they will loan you money on the house. You cannot get money loaned to you on the stock market. Additionally, he suggests looking at the historical ROI of real estate and the tax advantages.

Ethan wants all of his houses close together — within a mile of each other. He wants the roof and furnace to be good and for the house to have a maintenance-free exterior. He will only pay 80 percent LTV.

He also is not worried about earning a profit from his homes right now. "My properties are breaking even. If I can buy a property for $80,000 and it rents for $800, I can break even. It is a retirement plan. I figure that 30 homes at $1,000 a month is $30,000 a month minus repairs, vacancies, taxes, and other expenses. That will leave me with a $10,000 to $15,000 positive cash flow. At that point, I will own the homes outright."

His best experience was owning a house at 947 Ballard and finding out that the owner of 943 Ballard had lost her house to the bank. "I got it — right next to the one I have, and I got it for less than the one I bought first five years ago."

Ethan learned of the sale from someone who knew he invested in homes. That is why Ethan's motto is "It is not who you know, but who knows you."

INVESTOR INSIGHT:

It is imperative that you have good credit to get started so that you can get the best deals out there.

Seller Financing

When a seller helps to finance a real estate transaction by providing finances to the buyer, it is called seller financing. A seller can take a second note on the property or finance the entire purchase price.

Seller financing is different than traditional lending because the seller will not give you cash to complete your purchase. Instead, the seller extends a credit against the purchase of his home and you execute a promissory note to them.

The interest that will be charged by an owner is negotiable. Most owner-financed loans do not cost as much as traditional loans because there are no point fees. However, an owner financer will charge you enough interest for them to earn as much as or more than they would if they were investing in Treasury Bills or CDs.

Seller financing offers tax breaks for sellers and alternative financing for buyers who cannot qualify for conventional loans. So, if the seller does not need the cash from the sale to buy another home, they might be willing to take the tax break and interest on the money instead.

Not every home you find will have the option of owner financing. Sellers who make good candidates for owner financing are those who own their homes free and clear — they have no mortgage.

If you are looking for an owner-financed home, you will want to look at homes that are advertised that way. You will also want to look at homes listed that have little or no mortgage and then approach the owner with the idea.

You should also check into vacant and fixer-upper houses. Many people with these types of homes are ready to get out of the home owning business. They would be happy for you to give them some money down and then make payments monthly. It is far better than having a vacant home or a home in disrepair.

If you decide to try owner financing, you will want to keep a few things in mind:

- Do your research before making an offer. Just because an owner is willing to finance does not mean that the house is a good deal for you. Find comp houses in the area and crunch the numbers; only then should you make an offer.

- Be prepared to give the seller your credit report.
- The transaction time of an owner financed loan is fast since there is no formal loan process.
- Owner financing will save you money since you will have no origination fees or points.

Owner Occupied Loans

Most traditional home loans are owner occupied loans, meaning that you will be occupying the property after the loan is approved. Owner occupied loans have a more favorable loan rate than those obtained for investment purposes. However, you can get an owner occupied loan and use it for investment — simply live there for one year.

When you take out a home loan, the lender has you sign the occupancy affidavit stating that you plan to live in the home for at least one year. If you can live in the home for a year before renting it out, then you would qualify for one of these traditional loans.

Another way to get an owner occupied home is if you have a property with more than one unit and you plan to live in one of them. Though not a guarantee, many banks will consider you for the traditional home loan instead of an investment loan.

Home Equity Loan and Home Equity Line of Credit

A home equity loan is exactly how it sounds — it is a loan against the equity in your home. You can get a loan of up to 100 percent of your equity, but that costs more in interest and you must have good credit. A major advantage of the home equity loan is that your interest costs can be tax deductible.

A home equity line of credit (HELOC) is similar to a home equity loan, except instead of a loan in hand, it is an open loan that can be used as you need it. The interest rate of a HELOC is tied to the Prime Rate. You only pay interest for the amount of money you use, and the interest can be written off as a tax deduction. A HELOC is a good choice if you want to have money available but do not know exactly when you may need it or how much you may need.

Since you plan to buy investment property, you may as well use the equity in the home that you already have. It also makes sense to use that money to make the right purchase, even if you have to take a little longer to shop for the right loan later on.

❧ Been There, Done That ☙

Debbie Malone used a second mortgage to get her first piece of investment property.

"When we bought our first investment, it was with a second mortgage. Now, we use a line of credit. It enables us to put a lower cash offer on a property and close in days. This works well when you have a seller who needs to close quickly. If we are flipping the property, we renovate as quickly as possible to sell fast and pay off the line of credit. If we decide to keep it, we get a mortgage on the property, pay off the line of credit, and look for the next property."

Refinancing an Investment Property

Once you get a loan, you would still be wise to constantly consider whether refinancing your property makes good financial sense. You should always be on the lookout for better loan offers and constantly consider whether refinancing your property makes good financial sense.

One reason you may want to consider refinancing is to increase your cash flow. If you have built up equity in the property, you could use that equity instead of having it tied up. If you refinance to a lower rate or increase the term, your monthly expenses could also go down.

You can then use the equity to make improvements to your property, such as putting on a new roof, upgrading kitchens and baths, buying new appliances, or re-siding the house. You can also use the money to invest in more properties.

The major benefit of real estate investing is the ability to benefit from the equity in the property. If you have it, you may as well use it to increase your investment holdings.

After you have your loan, it is time to prepare the home to rent. In Chapter 7, we will explore the types of maintenance and repairs to expect and how to make repairs if you already have a tenant in place.

Tip Top Shape

As a landlord today, you will need to keep your investment in pristine order; you will also want to make improvements. Doing so will make a big difference in the profitability of the property.

You may need to replace windows or doors, add a new roof, replace appliances, replace or add siding, or complete a host of other projects. Although doing so costs some money, it will eventually generate big profits by allowing you to charge more rent and by causing the property to appreciate.

First, you must prepare a property for habitation. The property must be safe for renters. Cosmetic repairs, such as new paint, should be taken care of. Floors, fixtures, appliances, and windows should be clean. The exterior should be presentable. Garbage needs to be disposed of properly.

⊗ *Been There, Done That* ⊗

Rented.com CEO Andrew McConnell hears every story imaginable about renting experiences.

He recalls hearing about a condo owner in Florida who realized that his management staff was just not getting the job done. The dishes in the condo were filthy and unappetizing, and other parts of the condo weren't clean, either.

The condo owner decided he needed to resort to drastic action. Summoning all of the staff into the condo, he filled all of the supposedly clean glasses full of water and proclaimed a water break. "If they're clean, then drink!" he said.

The glasses were so dirty that none of the staff wanted to drink the water! Having proved his point and their subpar performance, the condo owner fired all of the current cleaning staff and found a new team.

Moral of the story? Be sure to check up on your cleaning crew regularly — your reputation may suffer if you don't.

Maintaining a property includes repairing units after old tenants leave and fixing problems while the unit is currently rented.

Finally, maintaining a property means adding those little extras that give your property more worth.

Ready or Not, Here They Come

As soon as you purchase your first rental home, you become a landlord, even if you have no tenants. You have to immediately think like a landlord and determine what needs to be done to your home to make it ready for your first tenant.

Let there be light

Even if no one is in the home, you will need to have the utilities on. You will need electricity and water to do all the cleaning and repairing. During the winter months, you will want the home to have electricity to keep the pipes from freezing. After the cleaning and repairing are finished, you will need the utilities on to show the home.

INVESTOR INSIGHT:

If you live in a cold area, have a plumber or electrician install heat tape on the water pipes in your investment home. When the temperature in the area where the pipes are located drops below a specified temperature, the tape, plugged into the electricity, will turn on and heat the pipes until the area surrounding the pipes has heated sufficiently to keep them from freezing.

Even if a tenant vacates the property, you need to be sure to keep the electricity and water turned on. Many utility companies offer a service to landlords allowing them to keep continual service, called leave-on service.

With leave-on service, the utility company knows that, when a tenant calls to cancel the service, it should be taken out of their name and put back into yours. Although this service does cost money for the switch, it does not cost as much as reconnecting each time, and it gives you peace of mind that the property will not be without electricity without your knowledge.

When you have the electricity in your name, you will want to turn off the breaker to the electric water heater to lower your bills when you are not using hot water for cleaning.

Prepare to prepare

Your unit may have remnants from the last owner or the last tenant. It will be up to you to get rid of the bed frame they did not take or the old sofa in the garage.

INVESTOR INSIGHT:

Know the laws in your area. Some states or local governments have passed laws concerning how long a landlord must hold onto items before they can legally dispose of them.

After you have gotten rid of the items left over, it is time to make a list of things to do.

Walk through each room, including the garage and basement, and write down what you see and anything you think needs to be done. Do the same with the exterior and yard of the home.

Make it shine

Your property is the product that your business is selling. As a landlord, the "sale" is either by month or by year, but you want to attract a "buyer" who will keep your property in good condition. You can attract the right kind of tenant and charge top dollar for your property if it is well taken care of. Cleanliness is key.

To save yourself time and money, take all your cleaning items with you. The time you save from having to go back and forth, and the money you will save by not buying items at a more expensive convenience store will be worth the effort to get your cleaning kit together before leaving home.

Here is a good list of cleaning items:

- Vacuum cleaner
- Broom
- Dustpan
- Mop and bucket
- Rags and sponges
- Cleaners and disinfectants
- Air freshener
- Toilet bowl brush
- Rubber gloves
- Trash bags

- Batteries for the smoke alarms
- Light bulbs
- Patching compound for nail holes
- Sandpaper
- Touch up paint
- Hammer, screwdrivers, pliers, and other typical tools

Some cleaning is obvious — take out the trash, sweep and mop the floor, vacuum the carpeting — but your tenants want and deserve more than that.

- Clean the walls of your unit to remove fingerprints and marks. If you allowed smoking in the home, you will also need to wipe down ceilings to get rid of tobacco smoke stain and the smell that goes with it.
- Clean appliances thoroughly, cleaning the grease and mildew off of refrigerators and stoves, cleaning the microwave, running the dishwasher to be sure that the inside is clean, and cleaning the oven.
- Clean kitchen and bathroom sinks and countertops, toilets, and tubs.
- Use bleach on discolored porcelain.
- Clean and shine all windows and storm windows.
- Clean garbage disposal and run a lemon through it to get rid of odors.
- Change air filters for the air conditioning and heating units.

INVESTOR INSIGHT:

Have your unit ready before showing it to potential renters. Applicants will notice the dirty floor or walls and will not want to rent — even if you tell them what you plan to do before they move in.

You may decide that hiring a cleaning agency is worth the price because they can get it done right and fast. You may have to spend two days cleaning the house, and a good team from an agency can get it done in an afternoon. That kind of time saving can be used to start looking for a good tenant.

Looking down

Carpeting is one area that you need to focus on. Check to see if it is spotted, worn, or outdated in style or color. You would not want to try to rent a house with gold shag carpet from the late '70s.

If you buy new carpet, look for something traditional in style and color. A small nap, tan carpet is a good choice. The short nap will help the carpet last longer, and the color will go with just about anything your renter owns in terms of furniture or décor.

If you have more than one unit, you will want to eventually have the same carpet in each unit. This strategy will help you out if you need a carpet remnant and will also keep the decision-making process easy.

If the carpeting is in good shape, you will want to steam clean it after spot cleaning any major stains, making the carpet look good and smell fresh. The goal is to get the unit rented as quickly as possible, and clean floors will help you do that.

Pesky pests

Pest control is part of the clean up process before renting to a new tenant. The best way to keep pests at bay is to exclude them in the first place.

- Seal cracks where pests can enter the home.
- Place insecticide, on a regular basis, around the foundation and soil.

- Use a residual insecticide in the house along the baseboards and windows.
- Use baits to get rid of ants.
- Keep gutters and downspouts cleaned out.
- Slope soil away from foundation to keep excess water from pooling.
- Keep trees and shrubs trimmed.

It may be in your best interest to hire a pest control company to eliminate pests and then make monthly or quarterly visits to the property to keep pests at bay. To find a good pest control company, you can look in the yellow pages or conduct a search on such sites as Angie's List. Be sure that they and their technicians are licensed. Also find out what pesticides they will use and ask for the least toxic one available.

Your tenant has the right to know about the pesticide treatments. They need to be given a notice before application. Check with state laws to determine how much notice is required in your area.

❧ Been There, Done That ❧

Dawn Cook relates her own pest escapade:

"We once had raccoons in the attic space of our commercial apartment and those creatures are hard to get rid of. We hired a trapper to catch them and he had to take them 70 miles away to release them. Apparently they can find their way back if you release them too close to the area that you removed them from."

Paint it pretty

Sometimes, no amount of washing will get rid of the stains or the dingy look of dirt. Painting the walls, ceilings, and any exterior wood of a home can make it feel brand new.

If you paint outside, be sure to use exterior grade paint. Keeping outside wood painted looks good, protects the wood, and makes the wood last longer. Consider using light trim on a darker colored home to make your home appear larger.

You may find that it is necessary to paint the exterior of the home or perhaps add new siding. The decision is yours to make, but do not assume that siding is significantly more expensive. Check the price of both and take into account that you will not need to do anything to the siding other than pressure wash it yearly, whereas, with paint you will need to repaint every five to 10 years.

A good tip when painting your rental unit is to consider a color scheme and then stick with it throughout the exterior and all the rooms. If you have more than one rental unit, stick with the same theme throughout. This tip will save you time and money with touch-up paint.

INVESTOR INSIGHT:

The only time this strategy does not work is if you have two units side by side. In this case, you will not want them to have identical exterior colors, but you can have the interiors the same.

Down below

Your basement is often where you will find the heating systems, water heaters, electrical panel boxes, and water pipes. You may also have a gas meter, oil tank meter, or sewer line in the basement. All of these must be checked and maintained on a regular basis.

You will also want to be sure that the staircase railings are secure and that the steps are sturdy.

Safe and sound

Safety is paramount where your tenants are concerned. If something happens to a tenant and it is due to something that was in disrepair or not up to code, you will be liable for their medical bills and can be sued civilly for damages.

Here are some things you should do when considering the safety of your tenants:

- Make sure faulted outlets next to sinks are grounded.
- Provide proper bathroom ventilation to prevent mold.
- Keep all smoke detectors in good working condition. Be sure to check your local laws to determine the number of detectors needed and the proper placement of these detectors.
- Make sure all doors have working handles.
- Make sure that windows can be opened and have working locks.
- Provide a fire extinguisher for the kitchen and check it every time you enter the home to be sure it is fully charged.
- Install a carbon monoxide detector if there is a fireplace or wood heater in the home.
- Tack down loose carpeting.
- Take care of exposed wiring.

- Let your tenants know what you would expect them to do in case of a fire.
- Replace door locks after each tenant leaves.
- Have the area around the home well lit at night.
- Abide by all local health and safety codes.

If you have a multi-tenant unit, you will also need to keep common areas clean and safe at all times.

Been There, Done That

Andrew McConnell warns that even keeping in touch with your renters won't necessarily save you from damages.

A homeowner who lets her house to short-term renters spoke to the renters on the phone. Everything seemed fine. She seemed to be talking to some responsible adults.

But then she got a phone call in the middle of the night.

Two parents had rented her property so that their kids could throw an after-prom party. Worse yet, they were serving alcohol, and some of the underage guests drank too much.

Several of the people renting the house had another short-term stay — in the hospital.

Curb appeal

Many building owners think about just that — the building. However, you own the entire package, which includes the building and the property surrounding it. Having the property look good will help you maintain high rents, attract good tenants, and raise the value of your investment property.

You will need to mow the lawn and trim the bushes. Caring for your property presents you as a responsible landlord and attracts good tenants who will help you keep the rent checks coming in.

CASE STUDY: NEAL BLOOME

Neal Bloome
Weston, FL
www.westonrealestatehomes.com
Premier Associates Realty LLC
(954) 608-5556

Neal Bloome is a realtor and a real estate investor in Florida. He is a hands-on landlord, along with his partner, who collects the rent, keeps the books, and pays the bills. He has subcontractors on his team who can handle repairs and maintenance.

As he gets ready to put one of his properties on the rental market, he makes sure that the unit is clean and that all appliances and services are in working order. Neal works mostly with Section 8 housing, which has some pretty strict rules.

"Section 8 housing, in a nut shell, is guaranteed rent from the government. It is for people who do not make enough income to live and pay rent. How they qualify will determine how much of the rent will be paid for them, but most is covered. In order for the government to be willing to subsidize the rents, they want to be sure that the apartments meet their standards."

If you wish to have your unit Section 8 approved, you will have to have it inspected. The inspector will examine the interior and exterior of the building, the plumbing and heating, the exits, each room, and all common areas to see if they are in good condition. The inspection must be made when the unit is vacant. All the utilities must be turned on and the inspector has to have access to the common areas.

The inspectors are trained to look for specific things found on the HUD form (see Appendix). For each item on the form, the inspector will mark pass or fail. If repairs are needed, that is noted on the form as well.

"For us, Section 8 housing has been both good and bad. It is good because you are assured of the rent each month, as long as the tenant remains in compliance with Section 8 laws. It is bad because we have seen more damage in our Section 8 rental units than in those that are not Section 8. Even with the damage, though, we have found this to be a good way to meet our financial goals."

When not using Section 8 as a source for tenants, Neal and his partner find and keep tenants the old fashioned way. When asked how he keeps a good tenant, Neal replied, "You need to be proactive to their needs and keep their rents reasonable. If you do these two things, keeping a good tenant is easy."

Repair While They Are There

Every investor of real estate needs to understand the benefit of repairing something as quickly as possible. Imagine a loose toilet. If taken care of immediately, it takes the simple tightening of a bolt. If you wait a bit longer, you will have to replace the wax seal at the base of the toilet. Wait even longer and you will have to replace the flooring around the toilet due to leakage. You may even have to replace the toilet if it breaks near the base. If the toilet is located in an upstairs bathroom, you will eventually have to repair the ceiling below. The damage only gets worse with time.

If the cost and extent of damage is not enough to convince you, consider your tenants. The goal of your investment business is to make money, and the only way you can make money is by receiving rent. If you let repairs go unhandled, you are going to lose tenants and be left with a repair bill.

Most state and local laws require that you maintain a rental property to a certain standard. Such standards include adequate shelter from the elements, heat, water, electricity, cleanliness, and sound structure. You will also be in charge of keeping your property up to date on local housing codes for light, ventilation, and wiring.

INVESTOR INSIGHT:

You can find out about local laws by going to your local housing authority or fire department. Be sure you know the code so that you are not penalized for violations.

If you do not fix items that need to be fixed in a timely manner, your tenant has several different courses of action he may take. For instance, he can withhold the rent, hire someone to make the repairs and take that off his rent, call the building inspector who will order you to make the repair, or even move out despite having a lease. Worst of all, he could sue you for discomfort, annoyance, and emotional distress. Even if he did not win, the

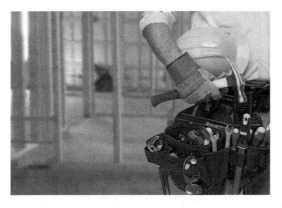

cost of the lawyer and the time spent in court could have been used elsewhere.

To make repairs on a unit, you have to have the tenant's permission to enter. Permission is not a problem when a tenant has contacted you with a problem, but there are times when you may want to make a repair they have not requested or when you want to make an inspection.

To enter the premises, you most often have to give a 24 hour advanced notice. (See Appendix for the law of your state regarding landlord entry.) The only time this notice is not required is in cases of emergency.

Emergencies include:

- Broken window, door, or lock
- Frozen pipes
- Water leak
- Suspected gas leak
- Fire

The best thing you can do is to handle the repair as soon as possible or have someone handle it for you. The rule of thumb is that major repairs like heating or plumbing should be addressed within 24 hours and minor repairs within 48 hours.

Just a Little Extra

Round and round

Ceiling fans in a room will make a good first impression on your tenants. They will also add light and help reduce heating and cooling bills. Ceiling fans cool the air by about seven degrees. If you use the fans in reverse

during the winter, it can bring the warm air from the furnace that rises to the ceiling back down to floor level, making you feel warmer without have to turn up the heat.

Choose the right sized ceiling fan for the room. Then, install it 12 inches from the ceiling to allow the air to circulate.

42 inches	up to 100 ft.²
52 inches	100 to 400 ft.²
56 inches	more than 400 ft.²

Open and close

Another way to spruce up a rental unit is to add mini-blinds to the windows. Mini-blinds look good and help conserve energy. If you have the blinds pulled against the sun in the summer, your cooling bills will decrease. If you have them open to the sun in the winter, your heating bills decrease. Having them in your unit sounds good when written in your classified ad.

Mini-blinds are inexpensive, can be bought at any local department store, and are easy to install. Have your window measurements with you when you go to shop for them. The best color for a rental unit is something neutral like cream or white.

Shutters

A good way to add spice to a building with little cost and no maintenance is by adding a set of shutters. If you purchase the plastic kind, you can install them with just six screws and about 10 minutes.

Shutters make a home appear larger, better kept, and even more expensive. They do not need to be placed on the back windows, but any windows on the front or windows seen from the road should have them.

White or cream shutters are best. They go with any color you have chosen for the outside of your home. If you have a white home, you may want to consider black shutters instead.

Say it with flowers

Adding a few simple flowers or plants to the exterior of your home can make it feel more welcoming. Put the flowers in the flowerbed or a pretty outdoor planter.

You do not have to know much about plants to make your home more appealing. You also do not need to spend much money. The good thing about adding plants is that, hopefully, your tenants will take care of them after they move in, and the exterior of the home will continue to look beautiful and inviting.

INVESTOR INSIGHT:

Be sure that you remove dead flowers during the winter months. A clean but empty flowerbed is far more appealing than one full of brown, dead weeds and flowers.

Give your kitchen and bath a facelift

When a home is for sale, kitchens and baths are a big selling point. The same is true when tenants are looking for a place to rent. Here are some inexpensive things you can do to these two rooms that will increase the value of your home in the future and allow you to gain more income now:

- Change the doorknobs or handles
- Paint stained cabinets white
- Put down new laminate flooring

- Install lighting under the cabinets
- Give the rooms a fresh coat of paint
- Add a kitchen island for more counter and storage space
- Update sinks to white or stainless if they have an outdated color such as harvest gold or avocado green

Having a kitchen and baths that look fresh and up to date will help you rent your unit faster and for more money.

Go green

Everyone wants to save money, including your tenants. If you do things to make your rental unit more energy efficient, you will attract more tenants, and you will increase the value of the property when you are ready to sell.

- Be sure the home is well insulated.
- Have the HVAC equipment checked regularly — systems that work properly are more energy efficient.
- When you purchase new appliances, purchase the energy-efficient variety.
- Insulate the doors and windows.

If you call your local electric company, they can provide you with pamphlets explaining what you can do to create an energy efficient home. Although not all the techniques are something that you can do as a landlord — it is not up to you to turn off the lights as your tenant leaves the room — you can learn about energy saving appliances and proper insulation.

In many areas, utility companies, nonprofits, or government agencies will help landlords create an energy efficient rental property through subsidies, tax breaks, and even grants.

When you have found the right rental home, have had it financed in a way that meets your financial goals, and have it clean, repaired, and ready to rent, it is time for a tenant. The next chapter will reveal how to find a good one.

Chapter 8

You Are the One That I Need

*I*f your rental property business is to be successful, you will have to maintain good landlord-tenant relationships. Finding and then keeping tenants will be your goal. This chapter will reveal how to successfully advertise for tenants and then screen them to see if the relationship will be a good fit.

Make New Friends, but Keep the Old

Finding good tenants is essential, but keeping the old ones will help you maintain a property with few vacancy bumps along the way.

When you buy a property, especially a multi-tenant property, you may "inherit" some old tenants. As long as there is nothing on their record to indicate that they make poor tenants, your goal should be to keep them.

Do tenants "transfer" with the property when you purchase the property? That depends.

If the tenants have a lease, then you purchase their leases with the property and have to honor that agreement. If the tenants do not have a lease or are leased on a month-to- month basis, then it will be up to you to keep the tenants or allow them to leave.

INVESTOR INSIGHT:

When you inherit tenants, you also inherit any deposits they paid and you will have to honor the return policy on those deposits.

Having a tenant transfer to a new landlord does not have to be difficult. For each old tenant who moves, you incur an expense, and so do they. Keeping them in their current place of residence is a win-win situation.

Moving is not just inconvenient; it is also expensive (and not just for the vacating tenant). Move-outs create landlord expenses, too. According to experts, bringing in a new customer can cost six times as much as keeping an old one — thus their gold status.

Determine what drew your tenants to the property in the first place:

- Amenities?
- Good service?
- Rent prices?

Understanding what your current tenants want and figuring out how to provide it for them is the key to keeping them.

Stop and Look

If you are purchasing a property with no tenants or you have vacancies to fill, a good way to let people know is to place yard signs on the property.

Yard signs are simple and inexpensive. They are also incredibly effective. Many of your potential tenants will come from the surrounding area.

Either they already live in the area and are looking for a new home or they live in the area and have a friend looking to find a place in the same neighborhood. It is even possible that someone just driving by on their way to somewhere else happens to see your sign.

The little signs from the hardware store can be used, but using a more professional sign will get you higher-end applicants. Consider purchasing the kind of sign that a realtor would use, with a solid frame that will hold up in the wind and will not deteriorate in the rain.

Your sign should have the words "For Rent" and your phone number. You may also put a website domain where you can have photos of the interior of the house or unit and a description of the amenities of the property.

You may also want to put out directional signs. These are signs at the end of the road that point to your rental. You have seen these types of signs used by real estate agencies and even yard sales.

Professionals and amateurs alike use signs, because they work. As you try to find new tenants, make signage a top priority.

INVESTOR INSIGHT:

Yard signs are especially effective if you live in a college town and will be renting to college students.

Put It in Print

In addition to signs, newspaper advertisements in the classified section are also a traditional way to attract new tenants. When looking for a place to rent, many start by looking in the classified section of the newspaper. Potential tenants who are out of town can log onto the online version of the paper and search as well.

INVESTOR INSIGHT:

Consider your target audience. If your typical tenant is a college student, for instance, then you might want to consider posting your ad with the campus paper, but be aware of the Fair Housing Act detailed below. If you post on campus, be sure to post in other locations as well.

Your ad should describe the benefits of your property and should contain an address, a price, deposit information, availability, and contact information. If you are not comfortable providing a complete address, provide a subdivision name or the section of town. Doing so will help limit calls to those who wish to rent in that area. Here are a few examples to get you started:

Simple:

2BR/1.5BA RENOVATED rustic home in Pinebluff. 1,300 square feet. New kitchen, bath, & wood floors. $800/month. $800 deposit. Application & lease required. Available June 1st. 555-555-1234

3BR/1.75BA brick home in Eagle Springs. Safe neighborhood with large yard. $1100/month. $1100 deposit. Available immediately. Call 555-555-1234

3BR/2BA Brick home w/central heat and AC, hardwood and tile floors, gas logs and garage. Convenient to SP & PH. Located off Morganton Rd. $1,250 deposit and per mo. Call Bob at 555-555-1234

Detailed:

This extraordinary condo has 1 bedroom, 1 bathroom, large living room, large kitchen, and a private veranda. Appliances include stove, refrigerator, dishwasher, microwave, A/C, electric heat, and a washer/dryer. Reserved underground parking space. Bicycle storage in garage. Close to Whole Foods, Harris Teeter, the Riler Park Bike Path, and the Riler Mall. No pets. $1,800/month and deposit. Available July 15. To learn more call 555-555-1234

Research Triangle Park condo. Easy access to downtown, transit, and the Capitol. In walking distance from the Center Street Mall and local downtown restaurants. Quiet community. Exercise facility. Come see this beautiful condo!!!! $1,650/month plus deposit. Available immediately. To learn more please call 555-555-1234

Your goal is to find tenants who are willing and able to make their rent payments in full and on time each month. You want someone who is likely to keep your unit clean and in good condition. You want someone who will follow your policies, but you need to be careful how you word your ads so that they are not discriminatory.

Federal laws prevent landlords from seeking out particular groups of people or disregarding others.

- The Civil Rights Act — You cannot discriminate based on race.
- Fair Housing Act — You cannot discriminate based on race, color, sex, national origin, family status, disabilities, or religion.

Most states and even many local governments have their own laws concerning discrimination and housing that go beyond the federal standards. In addition to those items listed in the Fair Housing Act, a locality may add occupation, sexual orientation, or citizenship status.

The Fair Housing Act has two specific provisions concerning the advertising of rental properties:

1. You may not make statements, written, oral, or even in pictures, that would indicate that you would rather have one type of tenant over another. You may not even imply a preferred number of children.

2. You have to post your ad either in a widely read newspaper or on widely read bulletin boards. You may not post your ad for limited group viewing only. If you wish to post to a specific, limited audience publication, be sure to post your ad in additional, more diverse publications as well.

Phrases to avoid include:

- Adult couple
- No children
- Spanish speaking
- Male only
- Close to XYZ Church

How do pictures enter into the mix? If you show a photo of your apartment complex, for instance, with people at the pool and the mix of people in terms of race are not indicative of the race of the population in the area, you can be sued for discrimination. Someone can suggest that by showing 60 percent Asian tenants in the photo, you are stating in pictures that you prefer to rent to Asian people.

If you show a photo during the holidays that has a Christmas tree, you can find yourself in similar trouble. You can be accused of discriminating against any religion that does not celebrate Christmas.

How can you avoid such problems? Here are some tips to keep your advertisements in compliance with the laws:

1. Review your ad thoroughly before placing it. If you think there is a chance that it looks discriminatory, start again.

2. Add the Fair Housing Logo to all your printed materials.

EQUAL HOUSING
OPPORTUNITY

3. Put a Fair Housing message in your advertisement.

"Landlord does not discriminate on the basis
of race, color, religion, national origin,
sex, handicap or familial status."

4. Only describe the apartment and the amenities. You should not state who you think would be happy renting from you.

5. Only use photos of the unit itself. Then, you will not have to worry about whether the people shown represent the make up of your area.

6. If you are not sure, leave it out. It is better to leave out a phrase and be safe than to find out you have written an ad in violation of the Fair Housing Act.

For further information on advertising and the Fair Housing Act, visit the HUD website at the following website: **http://portal.hud.gov/hudportal/ HUD?src=/program_offices/fair_housing_equal_opp/FHLaws/ yourrights**.

The Internet Era

Many rental property owners seek tenants via the internet. Posting on the internet is inexpensive, and depending on the site you use, can be completely free.

In addition to a low cost, internet listings have another benefit — space. With newspaper classifieds, the more you write, the more it costs. When you post online, space restrictions are removed. You will have the freedom to write as much as you think necessary.

To post on the internet, you can create your own website, create a blog, or find a site that allows you to post. If you have a large number of investment properties, a property with a large number of units, or a business that already has a website, creating a website for your properties makes sense.

If you do not have the skills necessary to create your own website or the price of doing so is prohibitive given your investment properties, you might consider creating a blog. Going to **www.blogger.com**, you can create a site in a matter of an hour and do not need any HTML skills. You simply follow the instructions, add photos and descriptions, and give your contact information. In the end, you will have a specific web address for potential tenants to view the property.

The problem with creating a blog is that no one will know it is there or be able to find it because it has no traffic and will not be in the search engines fast enough. Therefore, using a blog is a good way to supplement other forms of advertising. For instance, if you have a sign in the yard, you would be able to put the blog address on the sign and those interested in the property could find out more information.

INVESTOR INSIGHT:

If you choose to have a website or blog, use the web address on all of your advertising materials such as signs, other ads, and flyers.

Finally, you can find a website that will allow you to list your property. Some sites, such as **www.rentalhouses.com** or **http://rentbits.com** charge a fee for the listing. Other sites, such as **www.craigslist.org**, allow you to place your ad for free.

No matter how you choose to advertise online, there are certain elements that should be included in an online advertisement:

1. **Location:** Include the property address and list location amenities. What makes your property unique in terms of location? List all the location amenities. Rather than just say "Close to shopping centers," with an online listing, you can say, "Close to XYZ and 123 Shopping Centers."

2. **Rent:** State your rent. Better yet, state your rent with the median rent for similar properties in your neighborhood.

3. **Apartment features:** Include items such as number of square feet, number of beds and baths, parking, playground, fenced yard, basement, swimming pool, deck, patio, and hot tub among others.

4. **Utility cost:** Let your prospective tenant know what the average monthly bills have been for the last 12 months. You can also state which utility companies serve the area.

5. **Lease requirements:** List deposits that will be needed, including any deposit for pets. Also list lease restrictions such as non-smoking unit or need for renter's insurance.

6. **Lead Paint Disclosure:** Be sure to let your tenants know if lead paint was used in the unit.

7. **Vacancy date:** Let the reader know when the unit will be available.

❧ Been There, Done That ❧

Jane, an investor in Florida, had this to say about advertising.

"I paid to put my ad in a few local papers. The smaller paper seemed to get the most response. But in the end, I found my tenant from advertising on Craigslist. I try to buy homes that I would live in, so I advertised the way I would look for a place to rent. I would go to Craigslist.

"I do have a caution, however. Craigslist has scammers. People will call you with many sob stories. I had people calling to tell me about losing their job, being recently divorced, or having some other problem in order for me to waive the one thing I stated clearly in the advertisement — I would be checking their credit and past references.

"The first thing I told everyone who called was that I definitely would be checking landlord and employment history for the last two consecutive years with no exceptions. After I stated that clearly, the majority of people hung up the phone.

"I think that advertising somewhere like Craigslist is a good idea. It worked for me — I have a great renter who pays on time."

Let Me Tell You About...

Another good way to get tenants is through referrals. These referrals can come from friends, neighbors, and family. People who know you have a property for rent will often know of someone who is looking.

It is important, however, that you do not take referrals without checking them out as thoroughly as you would any other applicant. Your best friend may believe that John Smith would make the perfect tenant, but your best friend may not know the whole story.

If you have more than one rental unit, especially if you have an apartment complex, you might want to consider a referral program. This type of program gives your tenant a gift of some kind for every referral that results in a lease.

Such gifts can include:

- Gift cards to stores
- A prepaid credit card
- A free month's rent
- A check for a specified amount of money

Such incentives can help you find tenants similar to the ones you already have without much work on your part.

❧ Been There, Done That ❧

Debbie Malone had this happen to her:

"We rented to a young guy, who then recommended his mother and then his grandmother. We rented those three properties to all three family members for several years. What an easy way to get a good tenant!"

GPS of Rental Tenants

If you do not have the time to find your own tenants, you may want to consider having someone find them for you. Locator services are companies that can find tenants for any kind of residential rental unit, although some specialize in condos, townhouses, apartments, or single-family dwellings. You can find a locator service by looking in the Yellow Pages, often under the section "Real Estate Services" or "Rental Agencies." You would be wise to search online — a Google search should suffice — for tenant locator services in your area, as many of these companies are local in nature.

Locator companies represent many owners and have a consolidated list of vacancies in the area. Those looking to rent a home contact the locator company and are given a list of properties that meet their specifications, such as two bedrooms or near the transit line.

The service saves the renter the hassle of looking through all the different advertisements and saves you the hassle of advertising.

The property owner, not the renter, pays the fee to the locator company. Fees are about 50 percent of a month's rent, but if the company does not find a tenant for you, you will owe nothing. Depending on the rent of your property, this service may not be a good deal for you.

INVESTOR INSIGHT:

Using a locator service is more cost effective if you use a year lease since the price is low relative to the turnover ratio of your property. On the other hand, six-month leases or month-to-month leases increase the relative cost and may make the service an unwise choice.

Come On In

Having an open house is a good way to get people to see what you have to offer. If you do it right, you may only have to hold one open house to find your tenant. There is one big advantage to having an open house — time.

You will be able to show your property once instead of several times. If you have 10 people come through your open house in three hours, you are showing your house much more efficiently than if you had to show your property 10 different times.

Here are some tips to make your open house successful:

1. Market the open house through classified ads, yard and directional signs, and by letting any local organizations you belong to know of the open house.

2. Have all repairs complete before the open house. It is important that prospective tenants see the property as it will be when they rent it.

3. Provide cookies or other light snacks as a way to have a potential tenant stick around long enough for you to ask questions of them in a non-threatening situation.

4. Many tenants will make a decision based on the outside of the property. Be sure to have the entrance looking clean and nice. You will want to have the yard in good condition as well.

5. Have the unit clean and free from odors. Cleanliness includes freshly cleaned carpeting, windows, and appliances.

6. Set the thermostat in the unit so that those visiting will be comfortable. If it is too hot or too cold, they may wonder if the HVAC unit is working correctly.

Accepting Section 8 Tenants

Many landlords find tenants through the Section 8 housing program. Those who receive Section 8 get vouchers from their housing agency to help pay their rent. The federal government is in charge of the program and, therefore, in charge of the rent payment.

To accept Section 8 Voucher holders, you need to contact your local Housing Authority, and when you advertise, state that you accept Section 8 Voucher holders. But just because you accept these holders does not mean that they have to rent your property. Just as with any tenant, they may choose where they live.

You also need to understand that you, not the government, are responsible for choosing your tenants. Just because a tenant has a Section 8 Voucher does not mean that the tenant has been screened by the Housing Authority. You need to screen these applicants like you would any others.

According to the HUD site, "Once a PHA approves an eligible family's housing unit, the family and the landlord sign a lease and, at the same time, the landlord and the PHA sign a housing assistance payments contract that runs for the same term as the lease. This means that everyone — tenant, landlord and PHA — has obligations and responsibilities under the voucher program."

Tenants are obligated to:

- Sign a lease for one year
- Pay a security deposit if required by the landlord
- Comply with the lease
- Pay their share of the rent on time
- Keep the unit in good condition

The landlord is obligated to:

- Provide safe and sanitary housing as determined by the housing program's inspections
- Provide housing at a reasonable rent
- Provide all services agreed on in the lease

Now that you know how to bring in potential renters, you will need to know how to screen them and determine who is the right one for you. In Chapter 9, we will explore methods for qualifying your tenants.

More Than Just a Guessing Game

*W*hen it comes to choosing a tenant, you should not be playing a guessing game.

To get what you want, and to be fair to those who wish to live on your property, you need to establish a selection criteria. There are three general things you want when finding a new tenant:

1. Ability to pay in a timely manner
2. Willingness to abide by the lease and all the provisions in the lease
3. No sense that illegal activity will be engaged in on your property

Pay on Time, Every Time

As a landlord, you are a business owner, first and foremost. To be successful, you have to have tenants who pay the rent. Without the rent, your investment is not going to bring in a profit or, for that matter, break even. You cannot afford to rent to someone who cannot pay.

Verify income

The first thing you need to do is verify the income information provided by the applicant. This income will be in the form of a salary, social security, disability, and/or child support.

Income ratios

After you have verified the income of your applicant, you will want to look at their income versus their expenses. This income ratio is used by lenders to determine whether someone is able to handle a mortgage payment. Some experts say that a mortgage payment should be no more than 28 percent of gross income, and the mortgage payment combined with all other debts should be no more than 36 percent of gross income.

Say a mortgage lenders requires a 33 percent income ratio. To measure this ratio, multiply the applicant's gross monthly income (income before taxes) by 0.33. If the resulting number is more than your rent, they are above the ratio.

For instance, if you have an applicant who makes $2,000 per month, you would multiply $2,000 by 0.33 to get $660. If your rent is $600, they fall in the income ratio. If your rent is $700, it slightly exceeds the ratio. If the rent is $800, the rent is far above the ratio.

Of course, a ratio is just an arbitrary number. You need to use your common sense and gut feeling as well. If the applicant has an excellent credit history and good references, having an income ratio of 40 percent may not be a problem. But if the applicant's ratio is 29 percent but they have a history of nonpayment, you may want to ignore the ratio altogether in lieu of this information.

Credit check

You will want to check your applicant's credit history. A credit report can give you a detailed picture of your applicant's payment history to credit card companies, loan institutions, stores, doctors' offices, and other commercial enterprises. You can either get the report yourself or you can hire a tenant-screening specialist.

To do it yourself, you can order a credit report, for a small fee, from the following agencies:

Equifax
PO Box 740256
Atlanta, GA 30374
(800) 685-1111
Website: **www.equifax.com**

Experian
PO Box 2002
Allen, TX 75013
(888) 397-3742
Website: **www.experian.com**

TransUnion LLC
PO Box 2000
Chester, PA 19022
(800) 888-4213
Website: **www.transunion.com**

In addition to seeing the payment history of your applicant, you can also see how much debt the applicant has. To get such a report, you will need to have your applicant's social security number and a copy of the deed to your property. You will also need your applicant's written permission.

INVESTOR INSIGHT:

Many landlords charge a fee to the applicants to cover the cost of the credit check. If you choose not to do so, keep receipts of the credit checks you run, because the fees are tax deductible.

You can also check their history in a less traditional way, especially if the applicant is young and has not had the time to establish much in the way of credit. You can contact utility companies that the applicant has used in the past. If you cannot obtain this information from the company itself, so ask the applicant to provide you with documentation that the bills were paid on time.

Character Counts

When it comes to abiding by the lease and being a law-abiding citizen, you are seeking to determine the character of the applicant. Someone may pay their bills on time and have good income, but be someone who does not like to follow the rules or who has a criminal background.

To find out about an applicant's character, you will need to ask others who know him or her.

References

One of the best ways to determine if an applicant will follow the rules on the lease is by asking a previous landlord. If an applicant was willing to follow the old lease, you have an indication that they will do so for you. The same holds true for illegal activity.

When you talk to the previous landlord(s), ask the following questions:

1. Did the applicant pay on time?
2. Did they leave the unit clean and in good repair?
3. Did they give proper notice when moving?
4. Did they observe all the rental policies?
5. Did the neighbors have any problems with the applicant?
6. Were the police ever involved with the applicant on the property?
7. Would you rent to the applicant again?

Background check

If the applicant has never rented before, or you were not able to get satisfactory answers from the past landlord, you may want to consider getting a background check of the applicant. Companies that provide background checks can be found in the yellow pages. These checks take about three to 10 business days to complete.

As with a credit check, you will need to have your applicant's social security number and permission to conduct a background check.

Applicant interview

A good way to determine the character of someone is to talk with them directly. Ask them questions while filling in their rent application for them. In this way, you can see how they answer and if they look uncomfortable with any of the questions.

This strategy also gives the applicant a chance to clear up any possible information that might turn up in a credit or background check. For instance, if they were late on their rent for two months during a work related injury, you would feel more at ease with the information.

⅋ *Been There, Done That* ⅋

Marilyn Currie, CSP, of Claresholm, Alberta, Canada, has the following true story of an investment she had. It is a cautionary tale to all investors.

'Police invade home in residential neighborhood' scream the headlines, and a breathless announcer tells the world on the evening news. Unfortunately, the homeowners did not see the evening news and no one informed them. Not even the police or the neighbors.

Kids trying to break into the property told police of the pot growing operation. Police got the required documents, waited for the renter to return, and arrested him. Police then disconnected the electricity and water, confiscated the marijuana, and left. The grower was caught with cocaine in his truck, but was charged and released with a promise to appear in court at another date.

April 1 (April Fools' Day), the homeowner arrived to pick up the rent check and found a disaster. The back door was propped shut with a large board, the keys did not work in the locks, and there was no sign of the renter.

Apparently, the renter had moved back into the house and lived there for two weeks without utilities. The mess that greeted the owner was disgusting. One room was filled with garbage from floor to ceiling, hydroponics equipment covered floors and ceilings, the plumbing was plugged with dirt, and huge holes had been cut into the walls and floors to allow for ventilation.

The insurance company refused payment as they stated it was a criminal act and the perpetrator was given a fine and released.

Repairs were completed and the house sold at a loss. From the original down payment, loss of income, repair costs, and expected future profits, a total of $80,000 was lost.

Do a criminal check on the renter. It is your property and your investment, and you must be a good steward of that investment.

Your Standards

You will want to know what standards you are looking for in a tenant. After you have gathered the information, you need to compare that information to the standards you have set. Such standards include the following:

- **Income:** Set a minimum income, maximum income ratio, or maximum debt ratio.
- **Employment:** Set a minimum time for employment at the same job. Most lenders require at least two years at a particular job.
- **Residence:** Determine how long the applicant was at their last residence. Many landlords require that an applicant be at the last residence for at least two years.
- **Evictions:** Determine whether you will accept an applicant who has been evicted in the past.
- **Complaints:** Determine whether you will accept applicants who have had complaints from past landlords or neighbors.
- **Bad Credit:** Determine whether you will accept an applicant with bad credit.
- **Unverifiable Information:** Determine how will you handle unverifiable information.

❧ *Been There, Done That* ❧

Debbie Malone would never have guessed that the following scenario could happen to her:

"We rented a two-family unit to two sisters who did not get along. The police were there more than 20 times due to complaints over loud music and suspected drug dealing and prostitution. We never received a call from them, so talk to you neighbors; if you suspect something, check the police records. They were way behind in rent, dangling the 'accident settlement any day' carrot in front of my husband who took pity on one sister.

"They finally moved, owing thousands in rent. A few months later, we read about the quiet sister who broke into someone's house and attempted to kill them. She was sentenced to more than 70 years in prison."

The Application Process

When you know the standards you wish to follow and how you plan to find out the information that will help you get tenants with those standards, you need to think about the application process.

Here are a few tips to consider.

Treat applicants with fairness: You will need to follow the same procedure with each applicant interested in your vacancy. The best way to ensure fairness, and to help the applicants see that you are being fair, is to put your application policies in writing.

Require an application: Having an application will ensure that you get all the information you need to make a good decision regarding the applicant. Include the following on the application:

- Current address and phone number
- Social security number

- Length of time at current address
- Names and phone numbers of past landlords
- Name, address, and phone number of current employer
- Current income
- References' names with phone numbers and addresses
- Questions of importance to you, such as number of vehicles, pets, or water beds
- Statement authorizing you to contact references and check other provided information
- Statement authorizing you to obtain a credit report and a background check

INVESTOR INSIGHT:

Each tenant over the age of 18 should fill out an application. If you do not check everyone who will be on the lease, you may find that, although one person has good credit, the one who has been responsible for payments in the past does not.

The Time Has Come

The first thing you need to do when making the final choice for an applicant is to eliminate those who do not meet your written standards. For instance, if you want an income ratio of 33 percent, all applicants who do not meet this standard can be discarded.

After you have eliminated those applicants not meeting your criteria, you will have to decide between those who remain. Some landlords accept tenants in the order in which they applied. Others look at the applications more carefully, looking for further clues such as a glowing past landlord report as opposed to simply a good one, or an applicant who has held the same job for 10 years.

INVESTOR INSIGHT:

If you have more than one unit, you may want to keep the applicants on file for three to six months in case another opening occurs.

After you have made the decision, you will need to let the applicant know as quickly as possible. You do not want them to find another place to live before you contact them. If you find that they have already taken another rental unit, you can move on to the next applicant on your list.

It is also important that you turn down an applicant so that they can continue their search elsewhere. If you have turned down the applicant due to something found on the credit check, you need to give them the name of the credit bureau that provided the report. A letter you can give to such applicants is provided in the Appendix.

Finally, if you required application fees, all such fees for those applicants who were turned down must be returned. It is best to do so as quickly as possible to avoid any legal problems from applicants stating that you kept their money for a longer period than necessary.

CASE STUDY: DEBBIE MALONE

Debbie Malone
RE/MAX 1st Olympic Realtors
Lynchburg, VA
mailto: (434) 546-0369

Debbie Malone is a realtor and a real estate investor. When it comes to finding tenants, she is aware of the difficulties it can present.

When asked how she gets good tenants, Debbie replied, "We advertise in the newspaper and our work newsletter and by word of mouth from other tenants, but it is hit or miss. You can do all the right research, but sometimes it just does not turn out right. That is why I use a lease. This way, if I rent to a bad tenant and end up in court, I have documentation to help with my case."

Debbie uses a standard lease found at her local office supply store and says that despite being generic, it is sufficient for her needs; but she does agree that if you have specific issues you want to address, having a lawyer draft, or at least review, the lease before having a tenant sign is a good idea.

One way that Debbie helps to recoup any losses to a poor tenant is by collecting a deposit up front. Her policy is to collect a deposit equal to one month's rent. "If rent is $900 per month, we ask for the same amount for security. We tell them verbally and in writing that this is not last month's rent, it is insurance against damages. If the tenant moves without damaging the property, they get their full security back." If, however, the tenant leaves without paying rent or leaves with damages, the deposit will cover at least some of the cost.

Another thing that Debbie does to help encourage on-time payments is to charge a late fee. Rent is due on the first of each month and a late fee of $25 is charged after the fifth of each month. The lease states that being late three times in their lease period constitutes a breach of the lease agreement and the tenant will be asked to move.

Debbie says, "Make sure you tell them verbally and in writing what your policy is when you fill out the lease. Stick to it. We remind tenants that we have a mortgage to pay and if they do not pay rent on time, we have to come up with that payment from another source.

"We are not, however, without feeling when it comes to the payment of the rent. If the tenant is good and responsible and they hit a rough patch (medical bills or layoff), we work with them to allow them to stay even though they may owe back rent. As long as they are making the effort and they are upfront, we give them a break.

"We had a tenant who was laid off and got behind on rent. We worked with him for a year to get him on his feet. Two years later, he bought the house from us. It was a win-win for all.

"We had one tenant who rented for seven years, and another for 10 years. We have a Section 8 tenant who does the best she can, and she has been in the property for several years now. If you treat people well and help when you can, they respect you and treat your property well and try to do well by you.

"However, if you have tenants who are behind on rent and are avoiding you, they are not working with you, and they need to go. Get them out as soon as possible. Keep up with the correspondence and document everything.

"We have evicted several tenants over the years. It is nerve wracking the first few times, but it is not a bad process in Virginia. If rent is not received by the 5th, we send a demand for rent letter. If we have not received rent in full, plus late fee within five days, we file with the court and the sheriff serves the tenant. Most tenants receive the letter and move out before the court date. If it goes to court, most tenants do not bother to show up in court and the judge automatically rules in our favor.

"If the tenant does show up on the court date, the judge asks the tenant if they owe the money, and the judge says pay your landlord and get out in X days or the sheriff will physically remove you from the property.

"After the judgment, we go over to the sheriff's office for an eviction date. We have only had one tenant whom the sheriff had to remove. I think the tenant was shocked that they were being removed and they had not packed. The sheriff gave them five minutes to get whatever they wanted and waited for them to leave and told them not to return to the property. They were told to make arrangement with the landlord to remove their belongings. If they were not removed with 24 hours, their belongings became ours.

"We did have to go back that night because the tenant broke into the house. The police came and chased him out. They never called and we removed anything of value and sold it to recoup rent owed."

Despite having a few problem tenants, Debbie believes that real estate is a good investment. "Over the past 25 years, we have invested in the stock market and lost money, bought CDs and lost money, and invested in bonds and lost money. Nothing has given the return on investment that owning real estate has. We have purchased more than 45 properties, have never lost money on any of them, and we feel it is the safest place to invest."

Even in a soft market, she believes that real estate is a good investment. Others may be scared off and afraid of buying, and that is when you can potentially make a great purchase. "You can find undervalued property, fix it up, rent it for a few years, and turn a nice profit when the market improves. As far as I am concerned, there is no right time or wrong time to buy rental properties. It is about being able to locate the right deal and the right property for us and knowing where to look for it."

Even though Debbie owns 45 properties, she is a hands-on landlord, collecting the rent, doing the bookkeeping, and providing general maintenance, including painting and landscaping. Due to liability, she subs out any electrical and HVAC work and any complicated plumbing. She also contracts out roofers and contractors for larger repairs.

"When we purchase a property, we assess what it needs. We check the hot water heater. Many times, the elements need to be replaced, and sometimes the unit leaks. We find it better to spend the money up front and replace the unit (around $200) instead of having the tenant place a $75 service call.

"We check the plumbing fixtures, replace leaking faucets and outdated light fixtures, and change batteries in smoke detectors to make sure they are in working order.

"When we rent the property, we go over a property condition checklist with the new tenant. We list flaws and defects and have them sign a document regarding condition so we are all in agreement as to the condition. We also take photos. It is amazing how many times a tenant moves out and they say they did not damage the wall, carpet, or linoleum. If the condition is listed when they move in, it saves much aggravation when they leave.

"After a renter has moved out, we go in and assess the condition again. We allow for normal wear and tear, but if the property was just painted a year before and there are handprints all over the walls, if it is dirty, or there is damage or stains to carpeting, we assess a fee for repairs from their security deposit."

Debbie mentions two mistakes you need to avoid with your units. One is forgoing the annual or bi-annual inspections. You need to inspect your properties and address the problems as they come up. Do not wait until the tenant is moving out to make them pay for damages. If they break something a month into the lease, they should pay for it then.

The other mistake to avoid is forgoing the move-in inspection with the tenant. If you do not have documentation on the state of the unit, you will not be able to hold tenants to the repairs you have to do when they move.

Debbie understands the need for a good team of people for her investment business, and she understands that good subcontractors need to be on that team. In addition to subcontractors, such as a roofer, flooring installer, sheetrock finisher, and vinyl siding installer, Debbie has an accountant, an attorney, a settlement company, an insurance company, and a loan officer. She is her own realtor, but suggests that those investors who are not realtors should seek one out.

As a realtor, Debbie feels pretty confident when choosing a property. "If it is in a decent location and has curb appeal, we can expect to have a good experience with renters and that the property will appreciate. Having access to property info, I can assess whether it will be a good property or not.

"Location is the number one consideration. Physical condition is next. I always want to know how much money I will have to invest to bring it up to the condition we want. Price is third, and it can be negotiated based on the needs of the property.

"Being a realtor gives me an edge when finding a property, but the MLS is the number one way we find property. HUD and bank-owned (REO) foreclosure websites are the second, and word of mouth/FSBO are the third. We do not buy at auctions anymore — too much competition and the prices are driven up sometimes over what the property would have sold for on MLS."

Since Debbie understands real estate and the market trends in her area, she has invested in rental and flipped properties. "Some properties we buy with the intention of flipping, while others are long-term rentals. We just bought one property because it had a large detached garage and a ½ acre lot. We have been looking for such a property to store all of our rental equipment in one location. We bought another because it was in a neighborhood that our teenage daughter would like to live in one day. We used it as a 1031; it will keep paying itself down and we can gift it to her, avoiding the taxes."

Debbie believes that fixer-uppers can work for long-term investments and for flipping, depending on how much time you have to invest to bring the property up to a standard that would sell quickly. "If it requires much work that you have to hire out, it can cut into your profit. If it is more of a cosmetic update, you can get in and out quickly and flip it. I like the long-term investments that you can take your time on and make a profit and work at your pace."

When you have chosen your tenant, it is time to have them sign the lease. In the next chapter, we will explore the lease and the clauses and disclosures necessary to make your business more successful.

Chapter 10

The Fine Print

When it comes to landlord-tenant relationships, the lease is where it all begins. A lease or rental agreement is a contract between a landlord and a tenant. The contract gives the tenant the right to live on the property for a specific time.

A lease explains all of the tenant's and the landlord's rights and responsibilities. It states the terms of the lease including the rent, the length of tenancy, and any other rules specific to the property. A typical lease runs for one year, during which time the rent must remain the same and the tenant cannot move out unless you agree to the move.

A rental agreement is similar to a lease but does not specify a time. If you use a month-to-month rental agreement, you can change the rent with proper notification. However, without a lease, the tenant can also move elsewhere without the proper notification.

Written Versus Oral

There are two different types of leases — oral and written. Although both kinds of leases are legal as long as it does not extend beyond one year, it is wise to enter into a written lease or agreement.

An oral agreement can easily lead to misunderstandings and even problems over the enforcement of terms. You may have told the tenant that you will not allow pets, but if you did not write it down, you have no proof of that clause. Even the amount of rent your tenant is paying could be argued.

A written agreement means that the terms of the lease are bound by law and can be documented as such. A written lease provides you with the legal basis for enforcing the obligations of the tenant.

INVESTOR INSIGHT:

Make sure that everyone over the age of 18 who will live in the unit signs the lease.

What to Include

The content of your lease is up to you, with the exception of federal, state, and local laws regarding what leases can and cannot say. To learn of these laws before writing your lease, contact the governmental office in your municipality or county that handles landlord/tenant relations.

Most leases include the following information:

- Name and signature of landlord
- Name and signature of all tenants
- Date of signing
- Address of the unit rented
- The beginning and ending dates of the lease
- The rent amount and due date
- Procedure for collecting rent and late fees
- Returned check fees
- Security deposit and advance rent
- How security deposits will be returned
- Policy concerning security deposit as last month's rent
- Notice required to terminate the lease and where notices should be sent
- Disclosures such as lead based paint

A sample lease is available in the Appendix. Please note that this lease is for sample purposes only. Before you use this or any other lease, be sure that it meets your state and local requirements.

Because of the Clause

Many items listed on the lease are clauses. These are special items that are not true of all rental properties and may not even be true of each one of your properties. You have to be sure that any special policies you add meet with state and local laws. For instance, some states do not allow landlords to collect first or last month's rent. Others have deposit maximum limits.

You also cannot ask tenants to give up their rights. They have the right to have a safe environment with heat that allows no water to come in. They also have the right to get back unused portions of their deposit and be given warning before you enter the premises. Therefore, your lease will not hold up in court if you have asked your tenants to give up such basic rights.

You can require tenants to behave in certain ways as long as it is done within the law. For instance, you can ask them to keep the unit safe, keep it sanitary, or park in designated spots. You can also ask them to refrain from acting in certain ways, such as making noise that disturbs the neighbors, keeping pets, or using a grill on the balcony.

When you know the laws, you are free to choose the specifications of your lease. You may want to consider the following clauses:

Pets — Stipulate whether you allow pets and, if so, what kind.

Late rent payment — Stipulate the fine associated with late rent. You will need to address the actual due date of rent payments and the grace period before a late charge is assessed. You may also specify how many times a tenant can be late before more serious consequences occur.

Services as part of rent — State whether the rent includes water, electric, garbage collection, and/or phone service.

Renovation policy — State whether the tenant may paint, add wallpaper, put up railing, or add walls. Cosmetic changes are often allowed while major renovations are not.

Subletting policy — Stipulate whether subletting is permitted and whether it requires your approval.

Repairs — Explain to the tenant what to do in case a repair is needed. You can also lay out who is responsible for which repairs and any fees associated with specific repairs.

Renter's insurance — Stipulate whether you require renter's insurance.

Right of Entry — Detail when and how a landlord can enter a tenant's home.

Waterbeds — Stipulate whether you will allow a waterbed and whether it can be on the second floor. You can also stipulate that the renter must pay for all water damage due to a defective waterbed.

Others possible clauses include the following:

- Number of people per unit
- Parking policies
- Policy regarding illegal activity
- Attorney fees for evictions

To find wording for clauses such as these, you can go to **www.biggerpockets. com/rei/real-estate-forms**.

Written in Stone, Unless...

Although you have signed and dated a lease, you are able to make changes after it is signed. For instance, your tenant may have signed the lease and then decided to get married. She will need to change her lease to indicate her new last name and to add her spouse to the lease. Your tenant may be sent to another job location and need to sublet the apartment.

Any change can be made as long as it is done in writing and agreed on by you and your tenant. A sample letter stating a change in the lease is in the Appendix.

Hiring the Big Gun

As a real estate investor, you should make use of professionals who know their end of your business. One example would be the use of an attorney when writing up your lease template.

You can buy a template in any store, but you may find that the standard agreement does not work for you.

INVESTOR INSIGHT:

When you make a modification to an existing lease, make sure that all the blank lines are either completed or deleted. If you write in changes, they need to be initialed by you and by the tenant.

It is a good idea to hire an attorney who specializes in real estate law to prepare a lease for you, or at least look over the lease you have drawn up. Ask other landlords who they use. You can also get referrals from your real estate agent or your lender.

CASE STUDY:
DAWN COOK

Dawn Cook
Staged to Sell
(219) 513-8945
http://activerain.com/dawnc

Dawn Cook is a home stager and real estate investor in Indiana. Dawn finds her good tenants by screening carefully. Once she has a tenant in place, she keeps them happy by

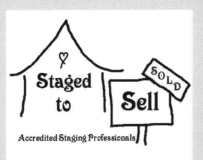

responding to their needs, keeping the rent fair, and giving them their privacy. If she has a bad tenant, Dawn says to "get your lawyer on it right away and get them out ASAP. I do not mess around with bad tenants — that can be a nightmare that will not end."

Dawn discusses a standard lease versus one drawn up by her attorney. "I have used both and I will never use a standard lease again, because there are too many liabilities; I have had an attorney who specializes in real estate law draw mine up. Be careful to choose a lawyer with experience and knowledge in this field."

The lease that Dawn uses with her tenants explains her security deposit policy. "I always get a security deposit of the full rent plus a $200 cleaning deposit; both are refundable 'if' the place is found clean and in good order. If everything is OK after the tenant moves out, both will be returned within 30 days after they leave the premises.

"I also explain my late payment policy. I do not want to encourage late rent payments, so I charge them $25 per day for the first day and $20 per day every day after until it is paid in full."

When Dawn had to evict someone, she was thankful to have her lease and her lawyer handy.

"I contacted my lawyer and had her handle it. I answered one call from the tenant and directed her to contact my attorney and informed her I would no longer be receiving her calls. My lawyer sent her a letter informing her to make any and all contact to her only (in accordance with the lease) and my lawyer got her out. It was a pain, but I am glad that I had a good lawyer I could trust to take care of it for me. I cannot imagine how horrible it would be to do it by myself.

Dawn shares her feelings about real estate investing. "I believe if you make good choices and are well informed, investing in real estate is an excellent way to make awesome amounts of money no matter your education level, status, or gender."

Lead Paint Disclosure

Since this information is so important, and so costly if done incorrectly, the information concerning the lead paint disclosure comes directly from the HUD website:

Congress passed the Residential Lead-Based Paint Hazard Reduction Act of 1992, also known as Title X, to protect families from exposure to lead from paint, dust, and soil. Section 1018 of this law directed HUD and EPA to require the disclosure of known information on lead-based paint and lead-based paint hazards before the sale or lease of most housing built before 1978.

Before ratification of a contract for housing sale or lease, sellers and landlords must do the following:

- Give an EPA-approved information pamphlet on identifying and controlling lead-based paint hazards ("Protect Your Family From Lead In Your Home" pamphlet, currently available in English, Spanish, Vietnamese, Russian, Arabic, and Somali).

- Disclose any known information concerning lead-based paint or lead-based paint hazards. The seller or landlord must also disclose information such as the location of the lead-based paint and/or lead-based paint hazards, and the condition of the painted surfaces.

- Provide any records and reports on lead-based paint and/or lead-based paint hazards, which are available to the seller or landlord (for multi-unit buildings, this requirement includes records and reports concerning common areas and other units, when such information was obtained as a result of a building-wide evaluation).

- Include an attachment to the contract or lease, or language inserted in the lease itself, which includes a Lead Warning Statement and confirms that the seller or landlord has complied with all notification requirements. This attachment is to be provided in the same language used in the rest of the contract. Sellers or landlords, agents, and homebuyers or tenants must sign and date the attachment.

- Sellers must provide homebuyers a ten-day period to conduct a paint inspection or risk assessment for lead-based paint or lead-based paint hazards. Parties may mutually agree, in writing, to lengthen or shorten the time period for inspection. Homebuyers may waive this inspection opportunity.

Follow the Law — All of Them

As a landlord, you are responsible for knowing state, local, and federal laws and regulations that have to do with rental properties. Failure to comply with a law can cost you fines or even lawsuits.

State laws deal with the following:

- Security deposits
- Landlord right of entry
- Housing standards
- Rental rules
- Repairs and maintenance
- Evictions

State laws that affect landlords can be obtained from your state's Consumer Protection Agency or Attorney General's Office. You can also find them at the library; in some states, they are available online.

Two good ways to find state statutes are to use a search engine specific to laws, such as **www.findlaw.com**.

INVESTOR INSIGHT:

Check for updates regularly, as laws can change whenever your state government is in session.

Local laws and ordinances should also be obtained. Local housing codes deal with the following:

- Structural requirements
- Plumbing standards
- Heating standards
- Health and safety standards

These laws can be found at your local building or housing authority, health department, fire department, or city manager or mayor's office.

In addition to the state and local laws, you need to be familiar with the federal laws. Federal laws include the following:

- Discrimination
- Environmental health hazards
- Landlord responsibilities

You can find these laws in the U.S. Code or in the Code of Federal Regulations. You can access the U.S. Code online at **www.law.cornell.edu**.

Fair Housing Laws

The Fair Housing Act (FHA) is the main piece of legislation that regulates multi-family rentals. It began as a way to provide fair housing throughout the United States by prohibiting discrimination.

The Fair Housing Act stipulates that no one can deny access to housing based on the following:

- Race
- Color
- Religion
- Sex
- Familial status
- National origin
- Handicap

States often have their own Fair Housing Acts that go beyond that of the federal government, including the following:

- Age
- Sexual orientation

- Personal appearance
- Political affiliation
- Place of residence
- Matriculation
- Veteran status

In addition to the lease of real estate, the law includes such things as advertising, interviewing of applicants, acceptance criteria, and renewal criteria.

Here are four steps you can take to stay in the bounds of the FHA:

1. Make policies based on wise business decisions.
2. Have all your policies in writing.
3. Let others who work for you know your policies and teach them how you want those policies to be carried out.
4. Be consistent — you must treat all applicants equally.

Are You Insured?

As a landlord, you are responsible for the safety of your unit. You can also be held liable for any accidents that occur. Therefore, it is in your best interest to have good insurance.

If you already have insurance, you may want to check your coverage to be sure that it deals with things common to investment property.

As with any insurance, there are differences in landlord policies and in the prices of these policies, but any policy you choose should include the following items:

- **Malicious damage by tenant** — This is all intentional damage to walls, doors, floors, ceilings, and outside structures.

- **Accidental damage** — This includes all those things that happen by accident, such as a washcloth getting flushed down the toilet by a two-year old.
- **Legal liability** — This is for expenses due to lawsuits, for expenses rising from a tenant who got hurt, or from property damage or loss.
- **Loss of rental income** — Sometimes damage, whether malicious or accidental, results in a loss of income while the property is restored to order. Loss of income can also happen if tenants default on their payments if hardship is granted to a tenant by the court or upon the death of a sole tenant.

Insurance premiums look expensive at first, but when you realize how much they can do for you, the price is well worth it.

There are many different types of insurance you can choose from. You will not need them all, but you do need at least liability insurance to cover you if someone is hurt on your property. You should also have basic property insurance to cover losses from fire or theft.

Other insurances you may want to consider include the following:

- **Tenant relocation insurance** — This will help your tenants with a move if your property becomes uninhabitable due to a disaster.
- **Flood insurance**
- **Bonding** — This will protect you against loss if you or someone you hire is robbed while they have rent money on them.

With the lease signed and the insurance in place, you will become a landlord. From that time forth, you will need to know how to keep your tenants happy and understand the administrative side of the business. In the following chapter, you will learn how to properly manage your tenants.

Chapter 11

Dot the i's and Cross the t's

Your job as a landlord is to have a professional relationship with your tenants.

This process begins when you have the tenant sign a lease. At this point, you need to be sure that your tenant understands the lease. Reviewing the lease is best done on a one-on-one basis, where you can answer any questions and listen to any concerns. One thing you can do to make your tenants aware of your expectations is to orient them to the property.

For instance, show them the different rooms and make sure they know how to use the appliances. Show them the breaker box and the water cut off valve in case of emergencies. Review the area's service, such as garbage collection, newspaper, recycling, and local utilities. Give them your number so that they know how to get in touch with you. All these things will help you get started on the right foot with your tenants.

While you are showing them around, it is a good time to perform a joint inspection of the unit. This way, you can both identify the condition of the unit and write down the condition and working order of the rooms and the appliances in the rooms. After you have written everything down, you

should each sign and date the list. A sample walk-through list is provided in the Appendix.

If there are items on the list that need to be fixed, get to them as soon as possible. After you have fixed an item, you can either checkmark the item on the list and have the tenant initial and date it, or you can create a new list of repairs that can be signed and dated.

INVESTOR INSIGHT:

Keep the original list and give your tenant a copy for their records. You might also want to take photographs of the condition of the house.

When the tenant moves out, this checklist may serve as documentation or evidence as to why you withheld all or a part of a security deposit.

Keeping It Straight

You have used a lease and a walk-through checklist. You have also collected the deposit and the first month's rent. It is time for a good record-keeping system.

For each tenant you have, you will want to keep a record. These records should have the following:

1. Rental application
2. Credit information collected during the application process
3. Signed lease
4. Signed inspection list
5. Payment history records
6. Repair completions
7. Any mail or email correspondence
8. Complaints
9. Repair requests
10. Records of conversations

You may need the financial documents for tax time; also, the documentation between you and your tenant can be used if you ever have to go to court over a landlord/tenant issue.

You will also need to keep business records. These records will help you do your taxes, determine whether a property is performing well, and determine when you can afford another property.

Such records include the following:

- Repair and maintenance receipts
- Advertising
- Car and truck expenses
- Contract labor

- Insurance
- Interest paid
- Legal and professional services
- Office expenses
- Supplies
- Taxes
- Utilities
- Wages
- Postage
- Computer hardware and software
- Any other expenses related to your business

You can keep all your files on the computer or you can create a paper system. Something as easy as an expandable file will work for receipts and a running total on rents paid. Or you can have a specific real estate investor software to do it all for you. Whatever you choose, just be sure that you keep everything and know where you keep it.

Hand It Over... Please

As per your lease agreement, your tenants will know how much rent will be charged each month. They will also know when it is due and where the payments can be made. As a landlord, you will have to decide which forms of payment you feel comfortable accepting — cash, check, money order, or any of the three.

INVESTOR INSIGHT:

If you accept cash, be sure to give the tenant a written receipt that has their name, the amount paid, and the date it was paid.

There are many different ways to collect the rent. One is personal collection, meaning that you go by each tenant's home and have them hand the rent to you directly. Personal collection often means that you have to set appointments and then hope that the tenant is there at the appointed time. The advantage is that you see the money immediately and know exactly who has paid and who has not.

You can also have your tenants drop off the payments in a drop box of some sort or at an office location. Be sure to specify exactly where the drop off is located and who can accept the check.

Having your tenants put the rent in the mail is also an option. The problem is that you are depending on the postal service to get the check to you. Tenants will put the check in the mail a day or two after it is due and it will not arrive for several days, or they will say that they put the check in the mail when they did not do so. The advantage is that it is a low-hassle way to collect the rent.

You may also provide your tenants with a deposit slip that they will take directly to the bank along with their payment. In this way, the payment is deposited immediately and you do not have to go to the bank to take care of it.

If you have a large enough tenant base, you might want to consider offering a draft service where you are able to draft their account at the first of each month for the rent amount.

❧ *Been There, Done That* ❧

Debbie Malone has a horror story to tell about people that were believed to be good tenants:

"We had a cute ranch on an acre that we did a lease/purchase for. Every month, the tenant would bring $700 rent in cash to our house. I told my husband he should go by the property once in a while to check on it, and he thought that if the guy was dropping off $700 cash, there would not be a problem. That was a big mistake!

"One day, the tenant called and said they were moving because they could not buy the house. My husband went by, and it was a disaster.

"Dirty is one thing — this was filthy. There were three layers of carpet in the living room all soaked with dog urine and feces. We had to have the floors refinished and sealed four times. In the basement laundry room, they left over two feet of wet, rotting clothing. There were needles strewn all over the inside and outside the house (he had hepatitis C — no wonder).

"The worst was the master bedroom. This home had an addition with a nice deck. The tenant thought this would be a perfect spot to tie their pet goat up. There was a foot of goat pellets that had to be shoveled out — by me. It was so gross."

So Long, Farewell

No matter how good of a landlord you are, you are going to have some tenants leave. That is simply the nature of the business.

If you have a month-to-month lease, the tenant should notify you in writing that they are going to leave. Your lease will have stated the terms of this notice, which is most often 30 days. If they do not give you notice, they will be obligated to pay rent for a full 30 days after leaving.

If you collected the last month's rent when the tenant rented the unit, by law you have to use this money for their last month.

If you have a longer lease and the tenant wishes to move, you have three choices:

- You can insist that they honor the lease by staying there or by paying for the unit until the lease is up.
- You can allow them to sublet their unit to someone else for the term of the lease.
- You can rewrite the lease to a month-to-month lease, allow them to give the 30-day notice, and then move.

After a tenant has stayed in a unit for the lease period, they have the option of moving. Most landlords specify in the original lease agreement that tenants will need to give a 60-day notice before the lease expiration of their intent to move when the lease is up.

If they do not intend to move, you can either have them sign a new lease or convert to a month-to-month lease.

INVESTOR INSIGHT:

In most states, if you accept rent after the lease has expired, you have automatically created a month-to-month lease. If you do not wish to go month-to-month, have the tenant sign a new lease before accepting any rent payments beyond the lease term.

Just as you followed a certain procedure when your tenant moved in, you need to follow one when they move out. You will want to let the tenant know how you will inspect the property, what deductions you will make from the security deposit for what repairs, and how you will get the remainder of the security deposit to them.

After the tenant has moved out their belongings and cleaned the unit, you will want to inspect the unit for cleanliness standards and for necessary repairs. If you have the tenant do this inspection with you, they will know how much is being charged and why. Have the tenant sign the report.

When you return the deposit to the tenant, send it to their forwarding mail address with a note detailing the initial deposit, the amounts deducted, and the purpose of those deductions.

✷ *Been There, Done That* ✷

Andrew McConnell recounts the horrifying moment when an owner of a California vacation rental found a message written behind a picture that had been hanging on one of her walls.

The message read, "You'll never know what went down in this house."

Fortunately, she was thorough enough at cleaning her property to check all of the walls.

And that wasn't the only damage. Sticky spots and other damage pointed to nights of questionable content.

A property owner needs to be ready for anything and needs to carefully examine his or her property when the tenants leave to make sure they haven't left any lasting marks.

Let Us Talk This Over

As a landlord, you need to understand that disputes with tenants are inevitable, but there are things you can do to keep these disputes to a minimum:

1. **Know the law.** Many disputes happen because one party or the other does not know the law. You may have written an illegal lease policy, or the tenant may not understand their obligation to follow the lease. It may even be something as simple as the tenant not understanding a particular clause in the lease.

2. **Stay calm.** Even if your tenant is screaming, you should remain professional.

3. **Discuss it.** You will be amazed how quickly some issues can be resolved simply by discussing them. There may be an easy solution to the problem.

4. **Meet with the tenant.** Rather than starting out with your lawyer, try talking with your tenant one-on-one.

5. **Get a mediator.** A mediator is a neutral third party who helps you and your tenant work out your differences. Some courts offer this service for free and sometimes Housing Commissioners have the authority to help.

6. **Get an arbitrator.** The arbitrator is also a neutral third party, but unlike a mediator, an arbitrator has the right to make the final decision. In binding arbitration, you agree before the start of the process that you will abide by whatever the arbitrator decides.

7. **Save everything.** Keep a record of everything that pertains to the situation. Any letters written, dates of any face-to-face meetings, police reports, or anything that will prove your case.

8. **Turn it over to a lawyer.** If doing all you can do has not worked, call your lawyer. Often, just getting a lawyer involved will end the dispute without it ever having to go to court.

The Check Is Not in the Mail

One of the biggest problems you will run into is the nonpayment of rent. Nonpayment can also include only partial payment of rent and any late charges.

If the rent is not paid on time, you must follow a legal procedure to get the rent. If you do not, and the time comes that legal proceedings must be held, you can end up in trouble with the law instead of your tenant.

Start by sending a late rent notice immediately after the grace period has expired. The late notice should inform the tenant of any late fees associated with his/her tardiness in payment.

If you do not hear from the tenant within two to four days of sending the notice, it is time to call the tenant. Let them know that their late fees are adding up. Also, tell them when the account will automatically go to your attorney for eviction proceedings.

If you get no response, you can send a warning letter from the attorney asking them to pay all rent by a specified day to avoid an eviction.

If the tenant still does not respond, you will have to start the eviction process. You can also report your tenant to the credit bureau reporting agencies.

Get Out... Now

You may have the best tenant screening process in the world, and yet you may have to evict someone. Eviction is the legal, forcible removal of a tenant from your property. Eviction is not pleasant and may well be the worst part of your job as a landlord. It is costly, it takes times, it can be complex, and it may need the services of your attorney, yet sometimes, it is necessary.

Evictions may become necessary as a result of the following tenant problems:

- Nonpayment of the rent
- Refusal to follow the lease and its provisions
- Engaging in illegal activity on your property
- Creating a nuisance problem
- Refusal to leave after the lease has expired

❧ *Been There, Done That* ❧

Debbie Malone's experience with illegal activity:

"My husband was refinishing the floors at a rental. He opened a closet door and found a pot farm! He called the police who set up a raid. We gave them a key so they would not break our front door. If you know there is something illegal going on, tell the police. If you let it go, or if they think you know what was going on, they can seize your home."

The best piece of advice for starting the eviction process is to start it immediately. The process is long enough on its own, so delaying will only cost you more time. Additionally, the longer a disgruntled tenant is in the unit, the more chance you have of sustaining damage.

INVESTOR INSIGHT:

If your tenant is involved in illegal activity, you can call the police and have them arrested, but starting the eviction process is still up to you.

Small Claims Court often holds evictions, but in some areas, they are handled by Housing Courts or Housing Sections of Superior Courts. Be sure to know which court your area uses before beginning the eviction process.

Eviction processes differ from state to state, but they all follow the same, basic steps. The steps listed in this section are only a guide. You will need to learn the laws for your particular area or have your attorney handle the eviction for you.

Even if you choose to use an attorney, it will be helpful for you to understand the main steps.

Serve Notice: You will need to serve your tenant with a notice. This notice is a document that lets the tenant know that you are starting the eviction procedure. It is important that this notice be served properly, so it is best to have a sheriff or sheriff's deputy deliver it. You can also use a company that deals specifically with serving legal documents.

You will also have to have the notice delivered to the court. You will need proof that you did so.

After the tenant has received the notice, they are then called a "tenant at sufferance." When it has reached this point, the court has control of the tenancy of the tenant at sufferance. The tenant has the right to remain until the court states otherwise.

Initiate the Proceeding: The notice will state the number of days a landlord must wait between the serving of the notice and the commencement of the eviction proceeding. After this time has passed, you will need to submit a petition to the court and pay a court filing fee. The petition will explain your reason for initiating the eviction and include the amount of money you believe is owed to you.

The court then issues a notice called a summons that demands that you and your tenant show up in court on a specific day. This notice will also have the petition attached.

Wait for Response: When the summons has been received by the tenant, they have to respond to the complaint within a certain number of days. They can respond by stating that the complaint is true, or they may respond with a defense as to why the complaint is not true. Their defenses may be that they already paid the rent, that they did not receive the notice legally, that they withheld the rent because you did not make repairs, that you are retaliating because they made a complaint against you, or that you are charging more than is due.

Attend the Hearing: You must show up at the hearing. If you do not, the case may be dismissed. If your tenant does not show up, it is likely you will win your case by default. Present your facts as objectively as possible, and do so in chronological order. Do not interrupt your tenant when they

are speaking and do not become argumentative. If the tenant says something untrue, make a note of it and bring it up when it is your turn to speak.

Get the Eviction Order: You will receive an order stating that you are legally allowed to remove the tenant from the property. If your tenant has appealed the judge's ruling, you may have to wait until the appeal period is over.

Remove the Tenant: You may have to have the sheriff remove the tenant from the premises. You may be required to store the evicted tenant's belongings, but this requirement varies by state, as does the length of time you need to store the items.

There are ways to make your business easier to manage, even with nonpayment of rents and evictions. The computer is one tool that can make the life of a landlord much easier. In Chapter 12, you will learn the various ways your business can be better by using a computer.

CASE STUDY: TAMMY KEMP

Tammy Kemp
First Impressions Home Staging & Interior Redesign
www.facebook.com/tammy.kemp.940

Tammy Kemp of Pennsylvania is a real estate investor with three properties, although she recently owned as many as seven. One reason Tammy has cut back on her rental properties is eviction.

"We do not want any more right now because, for the first time, we are encountering evicting a tenant and it has left quite a bad taste in our mouths. It is not a pleasant situation. We have found that our tenant needs to be evicted but is savvy as to how the system works. Before we take on more rentals, we will need to review our selection process and how to handle evictions more efficiently. Thankfully, we have a good attorney and recommend that anyone investing in real estate have one, too."

Despite this bad experience, Tammy wants to be an investor. She says that real estate investing will always be a good investment because people will always need a place to live. As interest rates go up and people have a harder time purchasing their own home, rental investing is even more desirable. Of course, she cautions that the only time you should buy is when the monthly rental income on the property will exceed your principal, interest, taxes, and insurance (PITI). "As for us, we never want to be put in an upside-down position."

To determine whether a house will meet the PITI requirements, Tammy and her husband split up the work. Tammy's husband determines whether the house is structurally sound. "We only buy a property if the work to be done is of a cosmetic nature."

Tammy makes the decision on the financial aspects. She and her husband decide whether the location is good. "Location is of paramount importance because that will determine the caliber of tenant willing to rent it. My husband and I keep our eyes open for signs of neglected properties and let our real estate agent know that we are always in the market if the price is right."

Since Tammy buys properties that are in good areas and in good condition, you would think she would have no trouble keeping tenants, but there are some issues. "We are in a Catch-22. We get good tenants by charging a higher than average rent in return for a better than average dwelling. However, the tenants who can afford the higher rent are usually just in between houses (renting while building a new home, relocating, etc.), so they never stay for more than a year."

Due to their choice of homes and the type of tenant these homes attract, Tammy prefers to use a month-to-month lease. This way, either party can get out of the lease whenever necessary. She found a standard lease in a book of landlord forms, but will be reviewing that lease in light of her recent eviction issue.

When Tammy is notified that a tenant will be leaving, she contacts them by mail immediately. "I send them a letter explaining what we expect the property to look like when they leave. It also contains an itemized price list for any repairs, replacements, or cleaning that we may have to do and lets the tenant know that the money will be withheld from their security deposit. You would be amazed at how clean our properties are when they leave. This only works if the property is immaculate and in good working order when they first start their tenancy."

Tammy also shares how she gets her tenants to pay their rent on time. "All rents are due on the 1st of the month, and we offer them a $25 discount if their rent is paid anytime before the due date. It is a win-win situation — they get to save $25 per month, and we get all the rents in at one time."

For Tammy, real estate investing is fun. She is thrilled when she takes a drab home and makes it shine. She has also been blessed to meet some nice people who, after they were no longer tenants, became good friends.

Chapter 12

Using the Internet

s a rental property owner and landlord, you are basically running your own business. And running a business these days without taking advantage of internet-based resources would be unwise. The good news is that you will find a lot of tools to help you online, including a lot of free tools.

Finances and the Web

At a minimum, you should consider online banking, which has improved considerably over the past five years.

- You can check your account daily to see what checks have cleared and what deposits have been put in.
- You can pay your bills without ever writing a check.
- You can transfer funds between accounts.
- You can balance your checkbook.
- You can open a checking or savings account.
- You can order checks.
- You can even get pre-approved for a loan.

Another big plus with online banking is that you can compare your current loan with new loan rates to determine whether refinancing is right for you. Online financial calculators make it easy to decide. You goal is to maximize your investment, so any refinancing that will help you achieve this goal is something you should consider.

Accounting

There are many different internet applications that can help your business with its accounting. These programs can help you keep up with expenses, income, bank balances, depreciation, tax records, and even help you keep your own income and expenses separate from that of your business.

Wave Accounting, for example, is a free service that is aimed specifically at small business owners, ideally those with fewer than 10 employees, which likely includes you. Check out **www.waveapps.com/accounting**. Other such programs include Turbo Cash, GnuCash, SQL Ledger and XTuple Post Books.

Other options include QuickBooks Online Plus, Xero and Zoho Books, each of which charges users a reasonable fee.

There are also many apps available for smartphones and handheld devices, such as FreshBooks and Mint.

INVESTOR INSIGHT:

Before you buy an accounting program, make sure the data you enter into the program is compatible with the software program your CPA uses at tax time.

Are You Connected?

The internet is an incredible way to have vast amounts of information at your fingertips. You can find Section 8 Housing requirements, low-cost energy saving tips, and stories of other landlords dealing with bad tenants, all on the internet.

But the internet can do much more than just be a glorified library.

CASE STUDY: DUAYNE WEIR

Duayne Weir
Investment Realities LLC/MarketLink
Real Estate Investment Specialist
http://activerain.com/profile/
duayneweir
(612) 363-2739

Duayne Weir, a real estate agent, investor, and contractor, believes strongly that a computer is a tool that you should use if in the business of real estate investing. "I have three websites — one for real estate as a realtor, one for investment real estate, and one for my contracting business. Today, if you do not have a website for your business, you are missing out on an online presence, a virtual storefront, and the opportunity for people to do research and find you credible! A website will help you be a success no matter what your business — real estate or otherwise. I enjoy building websites, and I think they should be a part of your real estate business; they will add credibility and profitability to your bottom line."

Duayne also uses his computer to keep track of income, expenses, and even to determine an ROI using a property analysis software program when looking at a particular property. "We use our software to tell us what looks good on paper. Of course, there is always some risk and some unknowns. My advice is just do your due diligence going into an investment, and always have an exit strategy."

Duayne finds his investment deals on the internet. He understands that it is a valuable research tool that will save him time.

Duayne is involved in real estate investing, because he believes it is the best way to invest. "Real estate is always a good investment. You always have an insured asset, unlike in the stock market. And unlike the stock market, you can always borrow against it. Any time is a good time to buy, but I actually like to buy when the market is soft. I find that there is much inventory and the pricing is low. The downside, of course, is that financing is tough during the slow times."

As a realtor and contractor, Duayne meets several of the requirements for investment team membership. However, he does not limit himself to his own expertise. "I work with other agents, and we mainly work with builders on new construction. I also work with several good mortgage bankers. I am a member of pre-paid legal, which does save me time and money when it comes to lawyers fees."

Other members on Duayne's team include a management company and subcontractors. One of the most important members of Duayne's team is a real estate tax accountant. "The tax benefits of real estate investing are the best of any investment out there, bar none. The government wants it that way so we will invest in real estate, because our whole economy revolves around real estate."

Duayne also understands that real estate investing is a good way to use retirement funds. "As long as you have a self-directed IRA and take full advantage of the 1031 exchange programs, using retirement funds makes sense. The most important thing, though, is to make sure you have the right professional assisting you."

Buy it, sell it, rent it

As discussed in Chapter 4, the internet is a wonderful way to find properties to buy and to sell properties you are letting go. You will have the option of searching national and local sites that are databanks of properties for sale. These sites are updated at least daily, and they can give you information faster than more traditional methods like the newspaper classifieds.

You can also get a better feel for the properties online than you can via print because words and photos are rather limited in print. Online advertising, however, gives the seller a chance to show multiple photos, give extensive details, provide video, interactive maps, and more to help you make a decision to see the home in person. Increasingly, many homeowners are choosing virtual tours as a way to show off their homes in the digital age. In fact, experts say such tours are critical pieces of all savvy marketing plans.

In many areas, companies continue to sprout up to create such tours for you. The options range widely. Some might simply choose a video that touches on the home's selling point. But more professionals seem to be choosing much more elaborate tours that are created with special software and scanners. By the time someone gets finished touring the home, they just might feel as if they've actually been there.

The field seems to be developing rapidly. Already, some real estate companies are developing next-generation virtual reality systems that can create truly immersive digital experience, allowing people to don special headsets to virtually stroll through properties.

Despite the rise of such technologies, for many people, a simpler approach to finding tenants will work out just fine. As stated earlier in the book, advertising online for tenants is a good way to get tenants quickly and inexpensively. Those who are looking for a place to rent, especially if you are renting to those 40 and under, will be looking online.

Supply buying is another use for the internet. Many stores offer online catalogs where you can place an order and have the products shipped right to your door. If you are in need of hardware, tools, or other items related to your investment business, ordering online may be a good place to start.

Some sites that may be of interest to a landlord include the following:

- **www.sears.com**
- **www.homedepot.com**
- **www.lowes.com**
- **www.walmart.com**
- **www.eBay.com**

Check them out

Learning as much as you can about your applicants is important. Using the internet is an easy way to get credit reports quickly. You can go to one of the three major credit bureaus to order, or you can join a service where you pay an annual fee and then a small cost each time you request a report.

Instead of ordering the report over the phone or by mail and then waiting seven to 10 days to see the results, you can order a report online and print it out instantly.

Chapter 13

The Tax Man Cometh

he purpose of the IRS is to tax net income. Net income is money you made minus money you spent to make that money. It sounds simple, but it is far from being so. There are more than 500,000 pages of income tax law text that you would have to know to be sure you are doing your taxes correctly. That is why it is so imperative to have an accountant who is knowledgeable about the laws that govern real estate investing as part of your team.

That said, knowing what your accountant will need from you and understanding the basics of tax law will help you run a better business.

The first part of taxable income is gross income — or how much you make. In the real estate investing business, rent is gross income.

There are exceptions to this idea of income. They include the following:

- **Loans:** If you receive a loan, that amount loaned to you is not taxable. The IRS makes the distinction as to whether there is a defined time for repayment and interest charged.

- **Gifts:** A gift or inheritance is not considered income and, therefore, is not taxable. The person who gave you the gift may have to pay a gift tax, though.

- **Leasehold improvements:** If a tenant makes changes to the property using their own funds, the value of that improvement is not taxable as income.

Now that you know what is excluded from income, let us look at what is included.

Rental Income

Any money you receive due to rent is taxable in the year it was collected. This technicality is particularly important for January rents paid in December, or collections that were due in November but were not collected until February.

This rule also applies to the collection of first and last month's rent. If you collect $1,000 in first and last month's rent in November of 2016, you will owe taxes on that amount in the year 2016. When the tenant moves out, in say 2018, you will use their last month's rent deposit but will *not* have to claim it as income because you already did so back in 2016 when you collected it.

Tenant-Paid Expenses

Ideally, you will never have to deal with emergencies while you are gone, but it can happen. If a tenant pays for a repair, that payment is considered income.

Trade for Services

If you are lucky and get a handy tenant, they may offer you their services in exchange for the rent or some portion of the rent. If you accept, you are going to have to include a fair market value of the services they rendered as income. For instance, if you have a tenant who lays carpeting and is willing to re-carpet a unit for you in exchange for his $650 rent, you will have to list $650 as income even though you never received any money.

Security Deposits

Unlike first and last month's rent, security deposits are not taxable while you hold onto them. The portion used at the end of the lease will be considered taxable income. For example, if you collect a $1,000 security deposit and use $800 of it to fix up the unit after the tenant leaves, you will only be returning $200 to the tenant. The $800 that you used must be declared as income.

Repairs Versus Improvements

Many landlords incorrectly assume that anything they do on their property is going to be tax deductible. The IRS makes a distinction between repairs and improvement.

Repairs are things that keep your property in good condition. These things include painting, fixing an appliance, and replacing a light fixture. These are deductions (see next section).

On the other hand, improvements to the property add value to the property and are considered income. You cannot deduct expenses, but you can recover your cost by taking depreciation. Improvements include such things as a new roof, new appliances, a deck addition, or the addition of a swimming pool.

INVESTOR INSIGHT:

To increase your cash flow, it is better to fix problems quickly and be able to deduct the price rather than wait until problems are so large that they require renovations and can only be recouped over a period of years.

Reduce That Income

In most cases, people strive to increase their income. At tax time, however, people are striving to reduce that income, at least on paper. As a real estate investor, you are no exception.

The second half of the IRS taxing formula of "income - expenses = taxable net income" is the expenses, also known as deductions.

Deductions come about when you spend money on your business, reducing your gross income.

Unfortunately, not everything you spend on your business is deductible.

If you spend $500 in postage for your business, that is 100 percent deductible. Spending the same $500 on business meals is only 50 percent deductible. Finally, spending the same amount of money contributing to a political fund that will help reduce property taxes is not deductible.

Rental income provides tax benefits that are greater than most other investments. These benefits will help you realize a profit on your property, but only if you take advantage of them.

Some deductions you will want to take include the following:

Interest: Many forms of interest are deductible if you are a landlord. These include interest from mortgage loans, interest from improvement loans, and credit card interest for goods and services used in your rental business.

INVESTOR INSIGHT:

To take the interest of a credit card off as a deduction, you will want to have a credit card used exclusively for goods and services of your properties.

Depreciation: You do not get to take the actual cost of a piece of real estate as a deductible in the first year you buy it. Instead, it is paid for over a specified number of years and is called depreciation. Depreciation will be explained further later in the chapter.

Repairs: Repairs for what the IRS calls "ordinary, necessary, and reasonable in amount" are deductible in the year that they were sustained. Repairs include re-painting, fixing floors, fixing gutters, fixing the roof (but not complete re-roofing), replacing broken windows, repairing appliances, fixing holes in the walls, or fixing leaks.

Travel: As a landlord, you are entitled to a deduction when you travel for any business related purpose. This travel includes going to your rental unit to talk with a tenant, going to the hardware store to buy a can of paint, or going to the attorney's office to have him check a lease.

You have two different ways to deduct travel expenses. You can deduct actual expenses or use a standard mileage rate. If you use actual expenses, you will need to keep accurate records of gasoline, upkeep, and repairs. To use the standard mileage rate, you must use it the first year you use your car for your business and you must not be deducting an accelerated depreciation on the vehicle.

If you travel long distance for your rental business, you can deduct your airfare, hotel bills, meals, and other trip expenses.

In general, you should stay abreast of the many mobile apps that are designed for people who travel on business. If you want help planning your trip, booking reservations, keeping up with expenses, monitoring gas prices, and so on, there is likely more than a few apps available to you at no cost or for a reasonable price.

Home Office: You may deduct home office expenses from your income as long as you meet certain requirements. To qualify, you must regularly use a part of your home exclusively for your business and you must either use your home as your principal place of business, meet tenants at your home, or have a detached building you are using as an office on your property. You will be asked for the square footage of space allocated to your business and then you will use form 8829 to figure the tax deductions allowable. By having a home office, you will be able to deduct a portion of your mortgage, utilities, taxes, and repairs on your home.

Employees and Independent Contractors: Any wages you pay can be deducted as a rental expense, especially if you are the true employer and are in charge of giving the employee a W-2, or if they are an independent contractor such as an exterminator.

Casualty and Theft Losses: If you have any damages due to fire or flood, you may be able to take a deduction for your loss or at least a portion of your loss. These types of losses are called casualty losses. The same holds true for theft loss. How much you can deduct depends on how much of your property was destroyed or stolen and whether you had insurance to cover the loss.

Insurance: Insurance payments are deductible for fire, theft, flood, and landlord liability insurance. If you have employees with health insurance and workers' compensation insurance, you can deduct the cost of these as well.

Legal and Professional Services: Any fees paid to your attorney or professionals such as property management companies, real estate investment advisors, or accountants are deductible as long as the work they performed for you was related to your rental activity.

Advertising: The cost of advertisements to find tenants or to find professional help are deductible.

Property Taxes: Landlords may deduct property taxes, and local taxes associated with street maintenance, sidewalks, sewer, or other community services.

Local Services: You can deduct the price of running water and trash collection if you provide them for your tenants.

Rental Items: If you rent furniture for the benefit of a tenant, you can deduct this cost. The cost of renting equipment like steam cleaners or pressure washers is also deductible.

Utilities: Any utilities such as heat, gas, or electric provided to your tenants are deductible.

Tax Preparation: It is wise to deduct the fees of your tax accountant. With all the laws and rules and exceptions associated with tax laws, having someone knowledgeable is worth the price.

It Is a "Loss" Cause

You now know your income and your deductions. It is time to figure your net income. If you subtract your expenses from your gross income and end up with a positive number, you have made a profit, and that profit will be taxed by the IRS. But if you subtract your expenses from your gross income and you end up with a negative number, you are operating at a loss — this is called net operating loss (NOL).

INVESTOR INSIGHT:

You can use your NOL against your income in another year or years. If you have a loss of $15,000 in year one, a profit in year two of $2,000, and a profit in year three of $13,000, you can use the loss from year one and use $2,000 of it in year two and the remaining $13,000 in year three.

But, of course, even net losses have IRS rules.

The IRS differentiates between passive and active participation. If you have only passive participation, you may not claim a loss on your business. For instance, if you are an out-of-town landlord who is not directly related to any day-to-day decisions in the business, you will not be able to take the deduction unless it is against a passive gain.

To be an active participant, you need to be involved in at least some of the following:

- Interviewing tenants
- Selecting tenants
- Dealing with tenant issues
- Repairs or maintenance
- Hiring out repair or maintenance work
- Supervising someone you hire
- Deciding which properties to buy
- Deciding which properties to sell
- Determining the rent to charge

In addition to being an active participant, you also have to show the IRS that you are a material participant, meaning that you own at least 10 per-cent of the property. If you only own 5 percent of the property with other people, you cannot claim the net loss.

Even if you hire a management company, you may qualify as an active participant. For instance, if you continue to approve tenants, set rent levels, and engage in the buying and/or selling of properties, you will be considered active.

Been There, Done That

Andrew McConnell tells the story of Gene and his wife, who already have busy professional lives in addition to managing their condo in the Shores of Panama Resort in Florida.

During the Great Recession, their condo lost a stunning $100,000 in value. Trying to recoup some of that loss while waiting for the market to recover, they began renting their condo out in 2007. Gene hoped to get back around 75 percent of their expenses and still enjoy the condo for themselves.

But his career as a mechanical contractor and his wife's career as a registered nurse didn't allow for the 8.4 hours or more that HomeAway — the owner of HomeAway.com, VRBO.com, vacationrentals.com, and numerous other vacation rental listing websites — estimates is necessary to care for a property effectively.

They found a rental company that the condo recommended. But they didn't make enough money to cover their expenses, and they continued to lose money on the property.

In fact, the management company was not only producing too little income but also providing poor service.

When Gene and his wife would use the condo as a vacation spot, they would have to spend at least two days of their vacation cleaning the home and doing repairs.

Gene knows he has a high standard. He doesn't like dust on the ceiling fans. A scratch on the wall is a problem for him. He's not being picky just to be picky — he wants his renters to feel like they're in a nicer place than their homes since they're paying good money to be there.

A chance ad on Facebook led him to Rented.com. Through their assistance, he quickly found an offer from a multi-region company that had a local presence near the resort. He was guaranteed $24,000 a year — 33 percent more than he was making previously.

He gets a check every month, the home is cleaned to his standards, and he goes down to the beach as soon as his vacation begins because he no longer has to loiter to make repairs. For five weeks each year, he can now go down to his condo and simply relax.

INVESTOR INSIGHT:

Talk with your CPA to be sure that the duties you perform will classify you as being an active participant for IRS purposes.

The second rule pertaining to net loss is deduction limitations. You are not allowed to deduct more than $25,000 per year as a net loss no matter how many properties you own. The number is even smaller when your income is more than $100,000.

If you have a net loss greater than $25,000, you can use it in subsequent years. You can also use any unused portion to reduce your capital gains when you sell the property.

Even though you have an overall net loss, you need to keep track of which properties had which percentage of the loss so that you can use the right amount of unused loss for capital gains. This loss is easy to track for many expenses like the following:

- Mortgage interest
- Property taxes
- Insurance
- Repairs
- Utilities

But some expenses are not unique to a property but are part of your overall business. For instance:

- Professional fees
- Office supplies
- Automobile expenses
- CPA fees

There are two ways to divide the common expenses: divide them evenly among your properties or assign to them an amount based on the percentage of rent versus overall rent income.

For example, if you have three properties and $3,000 worth of common expenses, you could just split the amount in three, meaning that $1,000 of the common expenses would be allocated to each property.

Or you can look at the rents of each property. In this example, Property A has a $1,000 rent. Property B has an $850 rent. Property C has a $1,250 rent. When added together, your rental income is $3,100. You can deter-mine the percentage of each by dividing the reach rent by the total rent.

Property A is $1,000 / $3,100 = 33 percent

Property B is $850 / $3,100 = 27 percent

Property C is $1,250 / $3,100 = 40 percent

So, to allocate the common expenses, you would give 33 percent of $3,100 to Property A ($990), 27 percent to Property B ($810), and 40 percent to Property C ($1,200).

No matter which way you choose to allocate the funds, keep complete records of what you did and continue to allocate in the same way in future periods.

The last major rule that affects taking a net loss is your Adjusted Gross Income (AGI). If your AGI is higher than $100,000, you have to reduce the amount you can take as a net loss. For each dollar you are over the $100,000 mark, you reduce your net loss deduction by $0.50.

For example, if you have an AGI of $102,000, you have $2,000 more than the allowable amount of income. You have to reduce your net loss by half of the overage, or $1,000. Your maximum net loss would only be $24,000.

Therefore, if your AGI is more than $150,000, you will not be able to claim any rental income losses. Instead, they have to be carried forward and used in years you do not have a high AGI or when you sell the property.

You can determine your AGI by looking on the line items of your IRS 1040 form, but when calculating your AGI for real estate deductions, things are not quite as simple. The modified AGI needed for real estate investment purposes does not allow most of the typical adjustments used to get the AGI.

Two, Four, Six, Eight, What Do We Depreciate

The next area of tax law you need to understand is depreciation. Depreciation means that you spread your expenses out over the useful life of the purchase rather than take the full deduction the year it was purchased. Depreciation is used on any property that has a useful life longer than one year. Property that meets this criterion is called a capital asset.

Assets such as these are computers, cars, tractors, and houses.

Useful life is when the asset has zero value. For instance, a car after a certain number of years has no book value. It may be of value to you, but it has no financial value.

With houses, however, useful life does not necessarily mean that, at the end of the depreciation period, the house will have no value. As long as you keep up the maintenance and repairs, the home is likely to appreciate in value. Depreciation is used as a way to deduct the asset a little at a time over a prescribed number of years.

Most assets are depreciated using the Modified Cost Recovery System (MACRS). Some assets can be written off using an accelerated rate and others, like real estate, have to use a straight line method.

The recovery period is the time the IRS states the useful life of the asset is. Comprehensive information is available from the IRS at: **www.irs.gov/pub/irs-pdf/p946.pdf**.

With the depreciation tax rules comes the ability to make certain elections, or decisions to use different methods of calculation. After you have chosen which one you are going to use, you have to continue with that method.

You can take your deductions over a longer time than is specified in the rules, which makes sense if your deductions are going to exceed the allowable limit. This strategy will, however, make your taxes even more complicated.

The amount of depreciation you claim in the first year you buy an asset depends on two things:

1. The type of asset involved
2. When you acquired the asset

The mid-month convention calculates your deduction for residential real estate. The half-year deduction applies to most of the other assets you own.

You will be allowed a percentage of depreciation based on the portion of year remaining after the purchase. Each year is broken up into 24 mid-months. So, if you bought a piece of property the first of March for $100,000, you would have 19 mid-months left, or 19/24ths of the year.

Then, to determine how much you would pay for depreciation in the first year, you need to know this number and the number of years the asset will appreciate, which is 27.5 years on residential real estate.

Here is how it would work:

$$19 / 24 = 0.79167$$

Divide this mid-month number by the depreciation years: 0.79167 / 27.5 = 2.879 percent.

Multiply the percent times the amount the building is worth, 2.879 percent x $100,000 = $2,879.

Instead of determining the percentage yourself, you can also find the percentages listed as a chart available in the Appendix. You can get more specific instructions by going to the IRS website, **www.irs.gov**, and printing the instructions for form 4562.

Other property is allowed to take accelerated depreciation over a five or seven year period. Accelerated depreciation can be at 200 percent or at 150 percent.

For these asset classes, the half year convention is used, meaning that the calculation assumes that the asset was placed in service in the middle of the year.

To find out the depreciation of an asset, you would divide the asset value by the number of years of depreciation (five or seven), and then multiply that by the percentage supplied by the IRS table in form 4562.

There is one big advantage to using acceleration — doing so produces a higher deduction in the early years, which can be helpful with cash flow. However, if you have already exceeded your net loss deduction, then you may wish to have it done in a straight line like your real estate.

There is one more thing to understand about depreciation. You cannot claim depreciation for land — only for the improvements on the land. To find out the cost of the improvements on the land, you can do one of three things:

1. Look at the assessed value of your property for tax purposes. This document will list the amount for property and the amount for improvements.

2. Look at an appraisal report. This document will show the current value of buildings and land.

3. Talk to your insurance agent. They identify the value of your improvements because they do not insure the land.

There is no one right way to depreciate your property. It all depends on what you are trying to achieve with your real estate investing business

It is worth saying one more time — talk with your accountant.

The 1031 Exchange

Sometimes, it is not possible to deduct enough income to keep your taxes at bay. Another thing you can do, besides reduce your tax liability, is to defer your taxes, or move them to a later year.

One such strategy in real estate is going through a 1031 exchange, which gets its name from Section 1031 of the IRS tax code. In a 1031 exchange, also known as a like-kind exchange, you essentially trade one or more properties for one or more replacement properties of like-kind, while deferring the payment of federal income taxes and some state taxes on the transaction. The bottom line is that you can use the proceeds from the sale of rental property to invest in another rental property without paying taxes on your capital gain. That is a huge benefit if you are expanding your business by investing in more valuable properties. Of course, you are not escaping taxes. You are merely deferring them to a later date when you no longer want to reinvest the proceeds from a sale into another property.

The reason behind a Section 1031 is that, if you own a property but re-invest the money immediately into another property, you did not get any economic gain — at least not the kind you could use to pay taxes. This situation is known as a paper gain — numbers on paper show a gain, but the money in the wallet is not there.

When you do a like-kind exchange, you have the same amount of investment, but the form of the investment has changed. For instance, you had two rental homes and now you have a duplex and a rental home, or you had three condos and now you have a six-unit apartment building.

Many people assume that this kind of tax deferral is used for large corporations or professional investors. The truth is that anyone can take advantage of this kind of exchange. You just need to carefully follow the IRS rules in the Internal Revenue Code Section 1031.

Here is a quick summary of the rules:

1. The original and the replacement property must be for investment purposes. If you plan to flip the property, it will not qualify for a 1031, nor will your personal residence.

2. The original and replacement properties must be like-kind. All qualifying real property located in the United States is like-kind. Property located outside the United States is not like-kind to property located in the United States.

3. The whole process has to be finished within 180 days of the sale of the original property.

4. The price of the replacement property has to be higher than the sales price of the original property.

5. Funds must go through a third party.

6. The seller of the replacement property has to sign stating that they agree to the like-kind exchange.

There are five different types of 1031 exchange. The simultaneous exchange happens when the original property and the replacement property are exchanged at the same time.

A delayed exchange is the most common type of 1031 exchange. Delayed exchange occurs when there is a time between the transfer of the original property and the gaining of the replacement property. This type of exchange has strict time limits.

The build-to-suit exchange concerns improvements or constructions, and it allows you to build on or improve the replacement property using the proceeds from the exchange.

A reverse exchange is when the replacement property is acquired while you have the original property. These are sometimes known as "parking arrangements." As with the delayed exchange, the amount of time that you can have both properties in your possession is limited.

Finally, there is the personal property exchange. Here you can exchange your personal property, real estate, or other assets, for like-kind or like class. You cannot exchange different classes — diamond rings for property — for example.

The 1031 exchange merely defers taxes. When you finally sell the property in a way that it is not part of an exchange, you will have to pay the taxes on the original deterred gain plus any new gain since the purchase of the replacement property.

You can find out more rules by going to **www.irs.com** and downloading form 8824 and publication 544.

Keeping the Records

Keeping records is a must if you want to take all the deductions available to you as a real estate investor. Without the records, you have no proof and that leads to some big problems where the IRS is concerned.

INVESTOR INSIGHT:

If you document each items as it occurs, you will be less likely to forget the information or lose the receipts.

For each expense you need to know the following:

- The amount of the expense.
- What the expense covers. It would be good to categorize it according to IRS category deductions.
- Who received the payment.
- The date the expense was incurred.
- The date the expense was paid.

There are some items you should file so that you can prove your expenses were warranted, allowed, and true. These receipts and other items will help you during tax time and help you in case of an audit.

Here are just a few items you should keep on file:

1. **All tenant information, all vacancies, and all the advertisements you place to find new tenants.** You will need to show proof that you intend to use the property as an investment over the long term. If you can show long-term leases, a low vacancy rate, and/or advertisements that show that you are seeking tenants, you will have proof that you are using the property as a rental and not just renting it until you sell it.

2. **Receipts — all of them.** To verify your expenses with the IRS, you will have to have receipts or canceled checks. Instead of shoving everything into a shoebox, you should have an orderly system that allows you to come up with everything you will need. For instance, you can have your receipts filed by category and in each category, have the receipts ordered by date. Keep receipts for insurance paid, service bills from plumbers and electricians, supplies, advertising, and agency fees.

3. **All depreciation.** Keep receipts of all improvements and all purchases of equipment. Keep the depreciation you have claimed in previous years as well. When you sell the property, the IRS will have you factor the depreciation to find the true profit of the sale.

4. **A car log.** If you use your car for business related purposes, you can deduct mileage, but only if you keep a detailed, written log. It is best to keep this log in your car. Otherwise, you will forget to write in it. The IRS does not want estimations. They do not want total miles, either. They want the beginning and ending mileage and the purpose and date of the trip. To make your log even more foolproof, log other trips in the car stating the same information but state that it was non-business.

Keeping records separate is imperative. Many real estate investors are part-time investors with other jobs. Small investors often use a home office for their work. It is easy to mix business with home under these situations, but you should be warned that if you do, you will not be happy with the results after an IRS audit.

The biggest thing you can do to separate home and business is to have a separate checking account and credit card for your business. Having a separate account shows the IRS that you are serious about keeping your home and your business separate. It will also help you since your statements will be more written proof about how much you spent, and where and when you spent it.

Even if you keep every receipt and read every book on real estate investing, you are not likely to be able to do your own taxes and get the deductions you deserve. An accountant will help you get the deductions, make decisions to help you with subsequent years' tax liabilities, and keep you out of trouble.

An accountant can do all of the following for you:

- Create a list of categories for which you can take tax deductions
- Tell you IRS limits on deductions
- Identify the IRS forms you need to submit
- Help you fill out the forms for an in-home office
- Keep repairs and improvements separate
- Advise you on which depreciation methods are best for you
- Help you make decisions about your future income and expenses with tax saving strategies
- Establish long-term goals
- Factor all the depreciation when you sell a property to determine the profit
- Keep up with changing tax laws
- Find deductions you did not know existed
- Identify problems early on
- Help with quarterly taxes
- And last, but not lease, prepare accurate tax returns

At tax time, every landlord should use an accountant.

If the fee bothers you, consider the alternatives — lost money in depreciation or an audit — and you will see that it is worth it. Best of all, the fee is tax deductible.

Net Loss Gets Even Better

Business entity

If you have not set up an actual company for your investment properties, you may want to consider doing so. The three main ways to set up a business for the purpose of real estate investing are the S corporation, the partnership, and the LLC.

The S corporation is a corporation that has its income taxes directly on shareholder returns. This type of entity will give less your personal liability if someone were to get hurt on your property, but it does not help in terms of taxes.

A partnership, on the other hand, offers tax benefits but does not protect you from personal liability. If someone gets hurt on your property, they can sue you, not just your partnership.

The last type of entity is the limited liability corporation (LLC). The LLC is a combination of the S corporation and the partnership; it offers personal liability protection and the use of good tax benefits. Before deciding on a business entity, talk with your accountant and attorney.

When you have an LLC, no matter what happens to the property held by the LLC, nothing can happen to your own personal assets. That means that, if someone sues because they got hurt on an investment property, they cannot come after your home, your car, your boat, or any other asset. The same is true for creditors of the LLC.

Advantages of an LLC

In terms of taxes, the LLC is far better than a corporation. There are several reasons why.

The first is that an LLC has pass-through treatment, meaning that the LLC is not a taxpayer. It just passes income, gains, losses, expenses, and tax credits to its owners. It is the responsibility of each owner to report his own share of the LLC income and loss on their own personal tax return.

INVESTOR INSIGHT:

An LLC does not have to have more than one member. You can own an LLC as the sole owner and get the benefits of having personal liability protection.

If you own the LLC as a sole owner, you will complete a Schedule C stating the income or loss you incurred as a member of the LLC.

If the LLC has multiple owners, it files an LLC partnership return, IRS form 1065. This form states the business activities of the LLC. It also allocates income, deductions, and other items according to ownership interests. Each owner then reports this allocation, or distributive share, on their personal tax return on Schedule E.

For example, assume there are three members of the LLC. Member A owns 50 percent while members B and C own 25 percent each. The LLC would file Form 1065 stating the activities of the LLC and would assign any income, deductions, tax credits, and other items at 50 percent for LLC Member A and at 25 percent for Members B and C. Then all three members do their taxes and report this percentage of income and deductions on their Schedule E.

INVESTOR INSIGHT:

State income tax rules for LLCs differ from state to state, but most states follow the federal tax treatment. States get extra money from LLCs by charging various fees. Some states charge a yearly tax on all LLCs, ranging from $250 to $800.

Many states also charge reporting fees that can amount to much more depending on the state. In New York, for example, the fee can run to a maximum of $10,000 depending on the number of partners in the LLC. Other states are much less expensive. The best thing to do is check with state agencies.

The biggest advantage to an LLC is that the owner of an LLC can use the net loss of the LLC as a deduction on their personal return, meaning that, if the LLC takes a loss, that loss does not have to be held over, but can be used immediately on your own personal taxes. You can use the LLC loss to offset your own income from other sources, even wages from an employer.

Limits on LLC Owner Net Loss Deductions

The tax law for LLCs does take into account your "basis" and imposes loss limitations based on such. For instance, if you have a rental property that has a net loss of $30,000, but you have a basis of $25,000, you cannot use the entire loss.

A tax basis is the money you put into your LLC. For example, if you put $100,000 into one rental property and $75,000 into another, and you are the sole owner of the LLC, your tax basis would be $175,000. Your basis is increased by loans you make to the LLC and loans used to acquire an asset. So, if you use a mortgage to buy a property, your basis is increased by the amount of the debt.

Continuing the example, if the LLC uses a mortgage of $250,000 to purchase another rental property, your basis would go from $175,000 to $425,000.

Losses are also limited by passive activity loss rules. Rental holdings are considered passive activities. According to the rules, you cannot have passive losses that exceed passive income. In other words, if you only take in $30,000 worth of real estate income, you can only assume that much debt. Anything above that passive amount has to be carried forward or used when you sell off your interest in the LLC. You are able to use losses that are $25,000 more than passive income as long as you do not have an adjusted AGI of $100,000 or more.

Real estate professional status

You can get around the passive loss rules if you are considered a real estate professional. To be a real estate professional, you have to spend a certain number of hours each year in real estate activities.

Internal Revenue Code Section 468 (c) (7) states the definition of a real estate professional. You must work at least 750 hours annually in the real estate business (about 15 hours a week), and you must spend at least half your time actively engaged in the real estate business.

You do not have to meet these requirements as part of an LLC. For example, if you work in the construction business, you spend half your time and the required hours working in a real estate field. If you qualify this way, you will also have to materially participate in the rental activity. That would make you eligible to take passive income losses greater than the passive income of your properties.

To be treated by the IRS as a real estate professional, you must attach that election to your tax return. After they accept that status, it cannot be revoked unless there is a change in your life to indicate it.

More than one LLC

You should get a separate LLC for each property.

One of the big advantages to an LLC is protection against personal liability. The LLC can, however, be sued. If you have a different LLC for each property, then a problem with one property cannot affect any of the other holdings you have.

If you already own a business and want to buy a piece of property, you can do so with your business entity, but it may not be a wise idea. If you buy the property separate from your business, you will have more flexibility in selling it in the future and you will not have any business liabilities affect the property.

Now that you understand taxes and the benefit of hiring a real estate accountant, you are ready to move on to the final chapter. In Chapter 14, you will learn how to use your real estate holdings as a retirement investment.

Rental Retirement

For many people, real estate investing is part of a larger plan — a retirement plan. You want to have a comfortable retirement fund. You want to have a steady flow of income on retiring. You want to be able to enjoy life, and you want to know whether it can be done using real estate as the tool.

If done, correctly, the answer is yes. Real estate investing can make you a tidy sum.

Real estate investing leaves you many different options. You can decide what you wish to invest in, and you can determine how those investments will work for you when you retire. Some of your options are as follows:

1. You could sell all your holdings and use that money as your nest egg.
2. You could keep all your holdings and use the rent coming in as your monthly cash flow to pay your expenses.
3. You could cash some of your holdings in and keep some earning income.

The only thing you have to decide is what mix is right for you.

If you decide to keep the properties as rentals after you retire, you can keep the money flowing in. You may choose to have someone else manage the properties, which will cut into your cash flow a bit, but depending on the number of properties you own and your cash flow needs, this may be a good solution for you.

If you choose to buy, rent, and then sell before retirement, you can use that money in a way that can create residual income for you by investing in vehicles that give you a monthly return.

Real estate investing has its pros and cons, just like any other investment vehicle. As a real estate investor, you will get to enjoy tax benefits and see your properties rise in value. You will be able to use other people's money to build up your own. Yet, you will have to worry about negative cash flows, slow markets, unruly tenants, and an investment that needs time to become liquid — you cannot sell a house as quickly as you can sell a stock.

For many people, the advantages outweigh the disadvantages, and real estate investing becomes part of a retirement plan portfolio.

❦ *Been There, Done That* ❧

Aziz Abdur-Ra'oof gives us this real life example:

"I have a friend who found out about a co-op in the same neighborhood with the United Nations. The co-op was 300 square feet and was selling for $100,000. That is not a misprint. Trust me, this is prime real estate.

"She financed $79,200, and since she had at least 20 percent down, she did not have to have personal mortgage insurance (PMI). The debt service costs her $6,403 per year. During her first year, she made $1,107, or 4.5 percent return. During her second year, however, she did not incur any closing costs, so she had $5,683, or 22.9 percent return. As the years went along, the rental prices increased somewhat and she went from a 25.3 percent return in year three to a 30.6 percent return in year five. Her five-year pretax average return was 22.2 percent."

If you had one of these deals each year for the next 10 years, you would make $7,500 cash flow per year per deal. That means that, after the last deal, you would have a positive cash flow of $75,000. Now, let us assume that you do not wish to be the one who maintains these 10 properties. You can hire a general repairman for $30,000 and make $45,000 with no hassles.

Rule of 72

There is an investing rule that lets you see how quickly your funds will double over time. It is called the Rule of 72. To find out how long it will take for your money to double, you divide 72 by the annual percentage rate you are receiving on a sum of money.

For example, if you have a property making an eight percent ROI, you can expect your investment to double in nine years (72 / 8). That means that, if you invested $5,000 on a $100,000 property, nine years later, that principal will have doubled to $10,000. But in real estate, that only accounts for the ROI that you are receiving in rent. Add to that the appreciation you will receive on the property in a nine-year period, and you will see an even larger increase.

Since 1968, houses averaged an appreciation rate of 6.34 percent a year. So in addition to earning $5,000 in rent income over the nine year period, you will have earned 6.34 percent for nine years and gained an appreciation value of nearly $35,000.

Imagine repeating this scenario with several different properties, each with $5,000 invested, and you can see how high the earnings can be.

Cash Flow or Appreciation Profits — You Decide

Before getting started in investing too quickly, you need to think about how you plan to use the properties. Do you want to buy and hold or do you plan to buy and sell? Either answer is acceptable, but different answers will require that you make different decisions when you buy your properties — decisions in what you will buy and how much you will spend.

Mistakes can easily be made if you are buying for one market, but making decisions based on another.

Looking at the buy and sell market, you will want to know the cost of repairs so that you can see if a home is being sold far enough below value for you to buy it, fix it up, rent it for a year or two, and then sell it. You will need to understand the difference between repairs that will provide good return quickly and those that will not. In some markets, adding granite countertops is a good way to increase the value of a home; in other markets, you would just be wasting your time and money.

There are other improvements that almost never add enough in additional value to even cover the expense, such as swimming pools.

If you plan to buy and sell, you need to buy properties that can be sold quickly and at a profit. When you are buying and then selling in a short time, under five years, you want to try to minimize your interest expense. Buying a property with a short-term holding plan that cannot increase in value quickly in five years and has a large interest rate loan will not be a good choice.

If you are holding property for the long-term, you need to understand long-term numbers. How much can the property support in rent? How much will the mortgage payments be? How many other expenses will the property incur? If you are buying to hold, buying a property with a negative cash flow makes no sense.

One of the biggest mistakes you can make is to assume that appreciation on the house will outpace the negative cash flow. It may not happen. Not to mention that you are losing money in the meantime. With houses that you intend to buy and keep, you want to have a positive cash flow as well as appreciation. If you start negative on the first count, you will never make as much positive on the second count no matter what the market does.

When you hold a property for the long term, you expect to earn profits immediately — just as soon as you can get a tenant situated in your unit. The ideal situation is that you achieve a positive cash flow, but due to depreciation and deductions, have a net loss. This way, you can enjoy the profits without having to pay the taxes.

Make the Appraiser Your Friend

When you plan to sell properties, either right away or in the future, you need to think about market value. Market value is the amount someone will truly pay for your house, and it can be affected by the following:

- Architecture
- Landscaping
- Neighborhood
- Convenience
- Other properties in the area

If someone wishes to purchase your property as a rental unit, other things that will affect the price include the following:

- Number of rental units
- Amount of rent tenants are willing to pay
- Likelihood that rent will go up

In the best of circumstances, the market value will increase by the time you are ready to sell simply because that is what property has historically done.

You can add to that increase through improvements. You can make the house have a higher market value by doing the following:

- Building an addition
- Replacing a roof
- Putting up a fence
- Adding a deck
- Paving a driveway
- Adding landscaping

There is no guarantee that such improvements will positively increase the market value of your home, but by observing other homes in the area, and the price of home sales in your area, you can make determinations about what will make your property have a higher market value and what will not.

One way to determine whether an improvement will increase the market value of your home is to think like an appraiser. What does the appraiser look for when he comes into your home and determines its price? Some things are beyond your control. For instance, you cannot change what the market is doing in your neighborhood, nor can you change the location of your property; but there are things he will look at that you do have control over, such as the following:

- Windows
- Screens
- Insulation
- Heating and cooling systems
- Kitchen appliances
- Garages
- Materials used, such as granite, compared with the rest of the neighborhood

Another way to determine what improvements will make the market value increase is to compare your home to the other homes in the neighborhood. If they have skylights and large decks, adding one to your home will likely

increase the market value of the home. On the other hand, if no one in the neighborhood has either, you are not likely to get buyers to purchase your house for more just because it does have those features.

Finally, you need to be aware of factors that are beyond your control. Such things can be supply and demand in your area, the economic health of the region, or even a new transit system that bypasses your neighborhood. Knowing about these factors can help you decide whether adding improvements will get someone to buy. If the economic health in the area is down and people are moving away to find work, no amount of improvements in your home will get them to stay.

In addition to thinking strictly of how you will use your investment properties to purchase your retirement, you can also think about how you can use current retirement fund monies to purchase real estate. A self-directed real estate IRA is the answer.

IRA Your Way

Traditional IRAs do not allow you to make key decisions concerning the investments of the money. You make a determination to have the money in this fund or that, but then you are left out of the loop until statement time.

A self-directed IRA gives you the chance to invest in ways that are not so traditional. It allows you to invest in an asset that you know and understand — real estate.

With a self-directed retirement plan, you choose your own investments, subject to various rules. The rules allow the account holder wide latitude, allowing them to invest in many types of real estate, including apartment buildings, office buildings, motels, residential rental properties and more. For many, the main benefit of a self-directed retirement account is that it allows a tremendous amount of freedom as well as control

While some people argue that self-directed IRAs and real estate are not a good match, mainly because of the complexity of it all, I beg to differ. True, there are IRS and other rules to be followed. But if you retain an accountant who knows the terrain and a competent plan administrator, you will likely fare just fine.

When using your IRA, you can form an LLC, a partnership, or even pool resources. All of these strategies are within the law and make investing through your IRA as easy as investing any other way.

Some of the tax benefits of real estate investing are lost, however, to IRA real estate investing. For instance, you cannot write off depreciation since you are getting your tax break by putting the property into a tax exempt entity.

Making It Self-Directed

When you choose to establish a self-directed IRA, you can do so by means of a traditional or Roth IRA. All self-directed IRAs have a trustee called an IRA custodian, an IRA administrator, or an IRA advisor. These trustees charge a setup fee and annual fees for their efforts.

Fees are quite different across different companies. The initial fee can be relatively low (some might even offer to waive the fee) or as high as thousands of dollars. Then, there are annual fees that you'll want to monitor. In general, fees vary widely because each trustee can do different things for you. The more they do, the more they charge you. A strong dose of comparison shopping will serve you well. Pay attention to the services that trustees will provide in exchange for their fees. Much of this information is disclosed on the internet.

IRA custodians merely hold your money for you and put it where you tell them to put it. They have the least expensive fees because they do the least for you.

IRA advisors do what custodians do and help you find properties, do all the paperwork, help you with legal documents, and much more. Their fees are significantly higher than that of a custodian.

Before determining which custodian, administrator, or advisor to use, check with the Better Business Bureau and your state's Attorney General's office. If you have friends using a self-directed IRA, see who they recommend. After you have narrowed it down to three or four choices, take all the initial paperwork to your attorney and have him look it over and explain anything that may be confusing to you.

While any form of IRA allows for real estate investment, there are other pros and cons to consider when choosing the account type best for you.

- A **traditional IRA** lets you deduct annual contributions from your income, but when you begin withdrawing money, those funds will be taxed as regular income.

- A **Roth IRA** gives you no deduction on your current contributions, but does allow you to withdraw funds tax free. If you expect to buy a real estate investment in an IRA and hold it for a long period, this is most likely your best option, particularly if the property increases in value over that period.

- A **SEP-IRA** is designed for self-employed individuals and small companies. This option is a good alternative for real estate investors who can make the higher contributions because they can build up funds more rapidly to purchase properties.

Be Vigilante About the Tax-Deferred Status of the Account

Once you have determined which type of IRA is ideal, you will want to focus on some basic rules to ensure that all goes well. It certainly can't hurt to talk to your accountant, plan administrator and others before you start making investments. The stakes are high: seemingly small mistakes can have consequences later on. The last thing you want, for example, is to be forced to give up your account's tax-deferred status or to be stuck with large penalties.

Remember that in order to maintain your tax deferred status, the entire transaction must be consummated via the self-directed IRA. Transacting from another account will ruin the investment's tax-free status.

As for the title, it must be in the name of the account trustee or the entity that actually holds the account.

Remember also that you cannot take profits prematurely from your self-directed retirement account. All profits must remain in your IRA account. Profits of course can be reinvested, but they cannot be transferred out of the account.

Do What the IRS Says

There are many rules governing the use of IRA funds. Such rules include but are not limited to the following:

- Properties held in your IRA cannot be your own residence. For instance, you could buy a retirement home, rent it to someone else, put the rental income in your IRA, and, when you retire, take the house as a distribution. Then you can move in.

- They cannot be purchased from your immediate family, but can be purchased from your siblings.

- You may not own the property purchased by your plan. It has to be owned by your IRA.

- You must ensure that your intended purchase is not a prohibited transaction. A prohibited transaction involves the improper use of your IRA holdings by you or any disqualified person. A disqualified person is any member of your immediate family (except siblings), employers, certain partners, fiduciaries, and other categories specified in the IRS code. Find a good advisor because IRS laws can be tricky.

- It must be for investment purposes only.

- Your business may not lease or be located in or on any part of the property while it is in your plan.

INVESTOR INSIGHT:

Using your IRA for real estate purposes can be tricky due to IRS laws. Because the laws governing IRA transactions are so complicated, you should consult with an experienced real estate professional.

Conclusion

Real estate is an excellent tool for building wealth, and rental properties are one way to do so. But the internet-driven industry is constantly morphing, and there is plenty of competition out there. With this updated 2nd edition, you will have an essential guide to running a sound rental business, one that will serve you well deep into your retirement.

No investment is perfect. Dealing with tenants, figuring out the tax laws, and dealing with repairs and maintenance can be a headache. It is up to you to determine whether the advantages outweigh the disadvantages.

Real estate investing is not a get rich quick scheme. You must understand the value of the many internet-based resources available to you, do your homework, be involved, and have a long-term investment plan to realize the most profit from the endeavor. Nonetheless, if you stick with it, you will realize high profits and be able to use that money to reach your financial goals.

This book contains the information you need to make an informed choice. You should realize by now that this is a business. If you are not committed to the process, you will not succeed.

If you do follow the plan outlined in this book, you have a good chance of making real estate investing work for you. You have the knowledge to begin investing in real estate. You understand what it will take. You are ready to buy your first property.

Happy investing!

Rental Agreements, Applications, and Forms

RENTAL APPLICATION 1

Date: _____

Application is hereby made to rent premises described as _____ for a term of _____ and ending the ____ day of _____, 20__, for which monthly rental shall be _____, payable in advance, and for which a security deposit of $ _____ shall be due before occupancy of the above-described premises.

A deposit of _____ is made herewith for the first month's rent, with the understanding that it will be forfeited as liquidated damages if this application is accepted and the applicant fails to execute a lease before the beginning date specified above, or if the applicant fails to pay the balance due as first month's rent. It is also understood that if this application is not accepted, or if the premises are not ready for occupancy by the applicant on the date specified above, the deposit will be refunded to the applicant at the applicant's request.

APPLICANT/SPOUSE INFORMATION

Name: _____ SS #: _____
Driver's License #: _____ State: _____
Spouse's Name: _____ SS#: _____
Driver's License #_____ State: _____

Number of children: _____
Number of dogs: _____
Number of cats: _____
Other pets, please state what kind and how many of each:

_____

ADDRESS INFORMATION:

Current Address: _____
How long have you been at your current address? _____
If less than 5 years, please give your previous address: _____
How long were you living at the previous address? _____

EMPLOYMENT INFORMATION:

Applicant:
Current Employer: _____
Employer Address: _____
Name of person to contact at your employment: _____
Contact Phone number: _____
Number of years employed? _____
Annual Income: _____
If you have been employed with this company less than 5 years, where was your former employment? _____
Name of person to contact at your former employment: _____
Contact Phone Number of Former Employment: _____

Spouse:
Current Employer: _____
Employer Address: _____
Name of person to contact at your employment: _____
Contact Phone number: _____
Number of years employed? _____
Annual Income: _____
If you have been employed with this company less than 5 years, where was your former employment? _____
Name of person to contact at your former employment: _____
Contact Phone Number of Former Employment: _____

REFERENCES:

Employer Reference: _____ Phone: _____

Personal Reference: _____ Phone: _____

Credit Reference: _____ Phone: _____

The information provided here may be used by the landlord or his agent to determine whether to accept this application. On written request within _____ days, the landlord or his agent will disclose to applicant in writing what kind of investigation landlord has requested, if any. If this application is refused, applicant will receive a written statement of the reason for the refusal.

Accepted _____ Denied_____

RENTAL APPLICATION II

An application should be filled out for each adult applying for tenancy.

Applicant: Be sure to fill out application in its entirety. No blanks should remain. The result of your credit history and reference check will be our main decision-maker on whether or not we will rent to you. Only those applicants who are responsible should apply.

Where did you hear about us?

❑ Newspaper   ❑ Signage   ❑ A Friend   ❑ Other: _____

1. PERSONAL INFORMATION:

Full Name: _____

Phone: _____

Work Phone: _____

Social Security Number _____-_____-_____

Current Driver's License #_____ State_____

Current Address _____

City _____ State_____ Zip_____

How Long? _____

If you currently rent, list your apartment name/location: _____

Landlord Name: _____

Phone: _____

Alternative Phone: _____

Current Rent Amount $_____
Why are you leaving your current residence?

_____

Previous Address _____
City _____ State_____ Zip_____
How long? _____
If you rented, list the name/location: _____
Landlord Name: _____
Phone: _____
Alternative Phone: _____
Rent Amount $_____
Why did you leave your previous residence?

_____

Current Employer: _____
Position/ Title: _____
How long have you been with your current employer? _____
Address: _____
Phone: _____
Gross Monthly Income *before deductions*: $_____
Other Income Amount: $_____ Source of other income: _____
Former Employer: _____
Position/Title: _____ How long with this employer? _____
Address: _____
Phone: _____
Why did you leave your previous employer?

_____

Are you a smoker? ❑ Yes   ❑ No

2. CREDIT REFERENCES:

This section may include bank accounts, credit cards, store credit accounts, etc.

1.   Bank Name: _____
      Address: _____City _____
      State _____ Zip _____
      Account Number(s): _____
      This account is a: ❑ Checking Account   ❑ Savings Account
                          ❑ Loan Account(s)
      Approx. Balance $_____ How long? _____

2.   Other Active Credit Account: _____
        Type of Account: _____
        Account Number(s): _____
        Expiration Date: _____
        Credit Limit: $_____
        Length of Account: _____
        All Payments Made on Time? ❏ Yes ❏ No

3.   Other Active Credit Account: _____
        Type of Account: _____
        Account Number(s): _____
        Expiration Date: _____
        Credit Limit: $_____
        Length of Account: _____
        All Payments Made on Time? ❏ Yes ❏ No

Have you ever been evicted from any residence? ❏ Yes ❏ No
Have you ever had a foreclosure/repossession (home, vehicle, etc)?
❏ Yes ❏ No
Date of occurrence: _____
If yes, please explain: _____

Have you ever filed for bankruptcy?
❏ Yes [❏ Chapter 7 or ❏ Chapter 13]   ❏ No
If yes, please explain: _____

Have you ever been convicted of a crime? ❏ Yes ❏ No
If yes, please explain: _____

3. PERSONAL REFERENCES:

(Please provide us with three (3) people (non-relatives that we may contact to verify your character.)

1.   Name: _____
        Relationship: _____
        Address: _____
        Phone Number: _____

2.   Name: _____
        Relationship: _____
        Address: _____
        Phone Number: _____

3. Name: _____
    Relationship: _____
    Address: _____
    Phone Number: _____

4. EMERGENCY:

Please list two relatives we may contact in case of an emergency.

Name: _____
Relationship: _____
Address: _____
Phone Number: _____

Name: _____
Relationship: _____
Address: _____
Phone Number: _____

5. OTHER INFORMATION:

Please list other persons who will be living in the residence, including any children.

Name: _____
Child or Adult: _____
Name: _____
Child or Adult: _____

6. PETS:

Name: _____
Type: _____
Weight: _____
Name: _____
Type: _____
Weight: _____

NOTE: Management MUST approve of any pets on the premises. A fee of $_____ will be required before any approved pet may be brought onto the premises. NO exceptions will be made.

7. AUTOMOBILES:

Please list all automobiles you plan to keep on the premises.

MAKE	COLOR	MODEL	YEAR	LICENSE PLATE#	STATE	MONTHLY PAYMENT

Desired Move-in Date: _____

Anticipated Length of Tenancy: _____

In order to process your application, a non-refundable $_____ application fee is required. This fee is due at the time you put in your application for processing and may not be waived for any reason. By signing below, you hereby agree that if you are approved for tenancy after review of your application, you will rent this residence. You also agree that if you are accepted for residency and you decide not to move in, any and all fees or rents paid will not be returned. The money retained will not be returned in order to cover costs associated with your decision not to rent this property as other potential tenants may have been refused tenancy. Landlord will need to pay for costs associated with re-advertising the property and reviewing other applications.

Your application will be processed in a timely manner and the results of our review will be delivered in one of three ways: telephone, fax, or via mail. Once your application has been approved, you agree to pay the remainder of funds due and complete all paperwork within _____ hours. If you do not do so, management will assume that you have elected to forfeit your reservation and deposit management will re-advertise the unit. If your application is denied, all money paid with this application will be reimbursed, minus the application fee.

Please attach a copy of the following required documents when submitting your application:

- Driver's License/Photo I.D.
- Social Security Card
- Most Recent Pay Check Stub(s)
- Most Recent W-2 Form OR Last Year's Tax Return

I declare that the application is complete, true, and correct and I herewith give my permission for anyone contacted to release the credit or personal information of the undersigned applicant to Management or their authorized agents, at any time, for the purposes of entering into and continuing to offer or collect on any agreement and/or credit extended. I further authorize Management or their Authorized Agents to verify the application information including but not limited to obtaining criminal records, contacting creditors, present or former landlords, employers, and personal references, whether listed or not, at the time of the application and at any time in the future, with regard to any agreement entered into with Management. Any false information will constitute ground for rejection of the application, or Management may at any time immediately terminate any agreement entered into in reliance upon misinformation given on this application.

_____   _____

Applicant's Signature   Date of Application

RENTAL APPLICATION III

This application is subject to the Landlord/Owner's approval. We require a separate application to be filled out for every resident over the age of 18.

THIS SECTION TO BE COMPLETED BY LANDLORD/OWNER
Property Address: _____
UNIT _____
Rental Term: _____ Lease (From _____ to _____)
_____ Month-to-Month
Amount Due Before Tenancy: $_____ (1st Month) $_____ (Last Month)
$_____ (Security)

THIS SECTION TO BE COMPLETED BY APPLICANT
Full Name: _____
Date of Birth: _____
Social Security Number: _____
Home Phone Number: _____
Work Phone Number: _____
Vehicle Information: _____ (Make)
_____ (Model) _____ (Year)
License Plate Number: _____ State: _____
Driver's License Number: _____ State: _____

Lessor's Disclosure of Information on Lead-Based Paint and/or Lead-Based Paint Hazards

Lead Warning Statement

Housing built before 1978 may contain lead-based paint. Lead from paint, paint chips, and dust can pose health hazards if not managed properly. Lead exposure is especially harmful to young children and pregnant women. Before renting pre-1978 housing, lessors must disclose the presence of known lead based paint and/or lead-based paint hazards in the dwelling. Lessees must also receive a federally approved pamphlet on lead poisoning prevention.

Lessor's Disclosure

(a) Presence of lead-based paint and/or lead-based paint hazards (check (i) or (ii) below):

(i) _____ Known lead-based paint and/or lead-based paint hazards are present in the housing (explain).

_____

(ii) _____ Lessor has no knowledge of lead-based paint and/or lead-based paint hazards in the housing.

(b) Records and reports available to the lessor (check (i) or (ii) below):

(i) _____ Lessor has provided the lessee with all available records and reports pertaining to lead-based paint and/or lead-based paint hazards in the housing (list documents below).

_____

(ii) _____ Lessor has no reports or records pertaining to lead-based paint and/or lead-based paint hazards in the housing.

Lessee's Acknowledgment (initial)

(c) _____ Lessee has received copies of all information listed above.

(d) _____ Lessee has received the pamphlet *Protect Your Family from Lead in Your Home.*

Agent's Acknowledgment (initial)

(e) _____ Agent has informed the lessor of the lessor's obligations under 42 U.S.C. 4852d and is aware of his/her responsibility to ensure compliance.

Certification of Accuracy

The following parties have reviewed the information above and certify, to the best of their knowledge, that the information they have provided is true and accurate.

_____

Lessor   Date

_____

Lessee   Date

_____

Agent   Date

RENTAL CONTRACT

Date: _____

Owner(s): _____
Address: _____
City: _____ State: _____ Zip: _____

Resident(s): _____
Address: _____
City: _____ State: _____ Zip: _____

The Landlord agrees to rent the dwelling located at
Address: _____
City: _____ State: _____ Zip: _____
to the Resident(s), known as: _____, for the
period beginning on the ____day of _____ (month), 20____, and
monthly thereafter until the last day of _____ (month), 20_____,
at which time this Agreement will end.

Resident(s) agree(s) to the following terms:

1. Rent:

Resident(s) will pay in advance on the first day of every month the amount of
$_____ as rent. Failure to pay rent on time will result in the Owner taking im-
mediate legal action to evict the Resident from the premises and seize the security deposit.

2. Late Fee:

Rent received after the first of the month will be subject to a late fee of 10%, plus $ _____
dollars per day.

3. Bad Checks:

Resident(s) further agree(s) to pay a service charge of $10 or 5% of the amount of any dishonored check, whichever is greater, regardless of the reason.

4. Security Deposit:

Resident agrees to pay a security deposit of $_____ as a guarantee that resident(s) will fully comply with the terms of this agreement. The Security Deposit may not be applied by the tenant towards unpaid rent at any time during the tenancy. At the end of the tenancy, Owner will deduct any damages, unpaid rent, or charges, and disburse the remainder to the resident.

5. Appliances:

Appliances located at or in the property are there solely at the convenience of the Owner, who assumes no responsibility for their operation. In the event that such appliances fail to function after occupancy is started, the Resident(s) may repair them at their own expense or ask that Owner remove them.

6. Pre-Payment Discount:

As an incentive to the Resident to be responsible for all maintenance of the premises and yard each month, and to make rent payments ahead of time, a discount in the amount of $_____ may be deducted from the above rental sum each month. THIS DISCOUNT WILL BE FORFEITED IF THE RESIDENT FAILS TO PER-FORM AS STATED ABOVE. If the discount is lost one month, the resident may still receive the discount in subsequent months by complying with the terms of this agreement. Discounts that are lost because a maintenance call by the Landlord was necessary during the month will be added to the amount of the next month's rent.

7. Extra Visitors:

Only the _____ adults and _____ children named below may reside in the dwelling.

_____

Resident(s) agree(s) to pay $75.00 each month for each extra person who shall occupy the premises in any capacity other than visiting.

8. Condition of Property:

Resident(s) accept(s) the condition of the property "AS IS," waives inspection of property by Owner, and agrees to notify Owner of any defects.

9. Loss or Damage:

Resident further agrees to indemnify Owner against any loss, damage, or liability arising out of Resident's use of the property, including visitors using the property with Resident's consent.

10. Cleaning:

Resident(s) accept(s) premises in its current state of cleanliness and agrees to return it in like condition.

11. Maintenance:

During the period of this agreement, resident(s) agree(s) to maintain the premises including woodwork, floors, walls, furnishings and fixtures, appliances, windows, screens doors, lawns, landscaping, fences, plumbing, electrical, air conditioning and heating, and mechanical systems. Resident is specifically responsible to replace and/or clean filters on HVAC units regularly. Any damages caused to units because of failure to change and clean filters will be paid for by the Resident. Resident will remove tacks, nails, or other hangers nailed or screwed into the walls or ceilings at the termination of this agreement. Damage caused by rain, hail, or wind as a result of leaving windows or doors open, or damage caused by overflow of water or stoppage of waste pipes, breakage of glass, damage to screens, or deterioration of lawns and landscaping resulting from abuse or neglect, is the responsibility of the Resident. Resident agrees to provide pest control if needed.

12. Vehicles:

Resident agrees never to park or store a motor home, recreational vehicle, commercial vehicle or trailer of any type on the premises; and to park only_____ automobiles described as follows: _____

Parking is allowed ONLY ON THE PAVED DRIVEWAYS PROVIDED. No vehicle may be repaired or stored on the property without a current registration and tag, except in the garage. ANY VEHICLE PARKED ON ANY UNPAVED AREAS OR WITHOUT A CURRENT REGISTRATION MAY BE TOWED AND STORED AT RESIDENT'S EXPENSE BY A TOWING SERVICE.

13. Pets:

Resident will pay a non-refundable pet fee of $_____ per month per pet. All pets found on the property that are not registered under this agreement will be treated as strays and disposed of by the appropriate agency as prescribed by law. A Resident(s) found to be harboring an undisclosed pet will pay a pet fee for the entire term of this lease, regardless of when the pet was first introduced to the premises. The Resident specifically understands and agrees:

A.   No pet that is attacked-trained or vicious, or known to have bitten people or damaged property, will be kept on the premises;

B.   Resident is solely responsible for any and all damage done by a pet to the owner's property including, but not limited to the premises, carpeting, draperies, blinds, wall coverings, furnishings, appliances, and landscaping, including the lawn and shrubbery;

C.   Resident is responsible for any and all damage or loss to persons or property of others caused by the Resident's pet(s) and agrees to hold the owner harmless for any such damage;

D.   All pet(s) will be cared for and maintained in a humane and lawful manner;

E.   All pet waste shall be removed and disposed of promptly, including waste deposited in neighbor's yards by Resident's pets;

F.   All pets shall be maintained so as to not cause annoyance to others.

14. Resident's Obligations:

The Resident agrees to meet all of resident's obligations; including:

A.   Compliance with all applicable building, housing, and health codes.

B.   Keeping the dwelling clean, and sanitary; removing garbage and trash as they accumulate; maintaining plumbing in good working order to prevent stoppages and/or leakage of plumbing, fixtures, faucets, and pipes.

C.   Operating all electrical, plumbing, sanitary, heating, ventilating, A/C, and other appliances in a reasonable and safe manner.

D.   Safeguarding property belonging to the owner against damage, destruction, loss, removal, or theft.

E.   Conducting him/herself, his/her family, friends, guests, and visitors in a manner that will not disturb others. Resident agrees to meet the above conditions in every respect, and agrees that failure to do so will be grounds for termination of this agreement and loss of all deposits without further recourse.

15. Subletting:

Resident agrees not to assign this agreement, nor to sub-let any part of the property, nor to allow any other person to live on the premises except those named in paragraph 4 above, without first obtaining the written consent of the Owner and paying the appropriate surcharge. Resident agrees that a failure to comply with the provisions contained in the Rental Agreement cannot be corrected after the fact; and that eviction proceedings may be begun at once without notice.

16. Court Costs:

Resident agrees to pay all court costs and reasonable Attorney's fees arising from the Owner's enforcement of legal action against Resident or any of the Owner's other rights under this agreement or any state law. If any provision in this Agreement is found to be unenforceable under the law, the remaining provisions shall continue to be valid and subject to enforcement in the courts without exception.

17. Owner's Statements:

All rights given to the Owner by this agreement shall be cumulative in addition to any other laws that might exist or come into being. A one-time exercise or failure to exercise, by the Owner, of any right shall not be construed as a waiver of any other rights. No statement or promise of Owner or his agent as to tenancy, repairs, alternations, or other terms and conditions shall be binding unless made in writing and signed by Owner.

18. Partial Payment:

The acceptance by the Owner of a partial payments of rent due shall not, under any circumstance, constitute a waiver of the Owner's rights, nor affect any notice or legal eviction proceedings commenced under state law.

19. Abandonment:

Resident's absence from these premises for 15 days while rent is due and unpaid, shall be considered abandonment. In case of abandonment, this agreement gives Owner the right to take immediate possession of the property and to exclude Resident(s) from entering the property; removing at his/her expense all his/her personal property contained in the residence and placing it into storage at Resident's expense.

20. Utilities:

Residents are responsible for payments of all utilities, garbage, water and sewer charges, telephone, gas, or other bills incurred during their residency. Resident(s) specifically authorize the Owner to deduct amounts of unpaid utility bills from their deposits after termination of this agreement.

21. Personal Property:

This agreement confers no rights of storage. The owner shall not be liable for any personal injury or loss of property by fire, theft, breakage, burglary, or otherwise, for any accidental damage to persons, guests, or property in or about the leased/rented property resulting from electrical failure, water, rain, windstorm, or any act of God, or negligence of owner, or owners agent, contractors, or employees, or by any other cause, whatsoever. Resident agrees to make no claim for any such damages or loss against owner. Resident will purchase the necessary "renters insurance" or provide self-insurance in adequate amounts to cover any risk. Resident agrees to list Owner as "additional insured" on any such insurance policies. _____ (initials)

22. Removal of Property:

Resident agrees not to remove Owner's property or make any alterations or improvements without first obtaining specific written permission from the Owner. Any removal/alteration of Owner's property without permission will be considered abandonment and surrender of the premises, and termination by the Resident of this agreement. The Owner may take immediate possession and exclude Residents from the property, storing all Resident's possessions at Resident's expense, pending reimbursement in full for Owner's loss and damages.

23. Waterbeds:

If any occupant of the premises uses a flotation bedding system, the Resident shall be required to carry an insurance policy with a loss payable clause payable to the Owner, covering personal injury and damage to the Owner, in a form standard to the industry, with a minimum limit of $100,000. If the Resident installs a flotation bed installation without securing the required insurance and providing the Owner with a copy as evidence, the Resident will be considered in default.

24. Termination:

After payment of one month's rent, this agreement may be terminated by mutual consent of the parties, or by written notice given by either party at least 15 days prior to the end of any monthly period. Owner may alter or modify any provision of this agreement by giving resident written notice at least 15 days prior to the end of any monthly period. All parties agree that termination of this agreement prior to _____ (date), regardless of cause, will constitute a breach of the tenancy and that in such case all deposits shall be forfeited in favor of the owner as full liquidated damages at the owner's option.

25. Method of Payment:

The deposit and first rent payment under this agreement must be made in cash, or with a cashier's check drawn on a local financial institution. Subsequent monthly rent payments may be paid by personal or business check until and unless a check is dishonored and returned unpaid. Whatever the reason, once a check has been dishonored, no other additional payments may afterward be made by check. Returned checks will not be redeposited. The Resident will receive 3 days' written notice and will be required to pay the amount due, including the bad check charge, in cash. Resident is aware that past rent, damages, utilities, or other costs owed by Resident may affect Resident's ability to obtain credit for future housing.

26. Delivery Of Rents:

Rents may be mailed through the U.S. mail to:

Address: _____

City: _____ State: _____ Zip: _____

Any rents lost in the mail will be treated as if unpaid until received by Owner. It is recommended that payments made by cash or money order be delivered in person to the owner's office at the above address. In order for the tenant to qualify for a discount, rents must be received by mail or in-person on or before the due date.

27. Return of Deposit:

Security Deposits will be deposited for the Resident's benefit in a non-interest bearing bank account. Release of these deposits is subject to the provisions of State Statues and according to the following terms:

A. The full term of this rental agreement has been completed.

B. Formal written notice has been given at least 15 days prior to the end of any monthly period.

C. Premises, building(s), or grounds have been inspected and there is no evident damage.

D. The entire dwelling, appliance, closets, and cupboards are clean and free of insect pests, the refrigerator is defrosted, and all debris and rubbish has been removed from the property; the carpets are cleaned and odorless.

E. Any and all unpaid charges, including pet charges, late charges, extra visitor charges, delinquent rents, and utility charges, have been paid in full.

F. All keys have been returned, including keys to any new locks installed while resident was in possession.

G. A forwarding address has been left with the owner.

The balance of the deposit will be sent 30 days after termination of this agreement to the address provided by the Resident, payable to the signatories of this agreement. If Owner imposes a claim on the deposit, Resident will be notified by certified letter. If such written claim is not sent, the Owner relinquishes the right to make any further claim on the deposit and must return it to the Resident, provided Resident has given the Owner notice of intent to vacate, abandon, and terminate this agreement proper to the expiration of its full term, at least 15 days in advance.

28. Phone:

If telephone land line is required, resident is responsible to install and maintain telephone service, and agrees to furnish to the owner the phone number, and any changes, within 3 days after installation.

29. Gas, Electric, and Water:

Resident agrees to transfer the gas, electric, and water service charges to his or her name immediately upon occupancy and to make arrangements for meter readings as needed.

30. Three (3) Day Inspection:

Under the terms of this discount lease/rental agreement, Residents will be provided with an inspection sheet. Resident will inspect the premises and fill out and return the inspection sheet to the Owner within 3 days after taking possession of the premises. If no defects have been reported after 3 days have expired, it will be assumed that the property and its appurtenances are functioning in a satisfactory manner in all respects. Resident agrees that failure to submit inspection sheet shall be conclusive proof that there were no defects of note in the property. After the expiration of the 3-day period, Resident is obligated to provide for routine maintenance at his/her own expense, or to lose the discount.

31. Owner's Agents and Access:

The owner may be represented by an agent who will carry identification. Resident specifically agrees to permit the owner or Owner's agent(s) access to the premises for the purposes of inspection, repairs, or to show the property to another person at reasonable hours, on request. Resident will also allow signage in the yard.

32. Repairs:

The monthly discount is offered as an incentive to maintain the property. In the event repairs are needed, it is urged to arrange for professional assistance in performing repairs that are beyond the competence of the Resident. Resident should refrain from contacting the Owner except for emergencies, to report leaks or other urgent problems that may cause damage to the property, or for repairs costing more that the discount because such involvement by the Owner will result in the loss of the discount. Any repair that will cost more than the amount of the discount must be approved in writing by the owner or the tenant will be responsible for the entire cost of that repair. Any improvement made by the tenant shall become the property of the Owner at the conclusion of this agreement.

33. Worker's Warranty:

Resident(s) guarantee(s) that the Resident will undertake work or repairs only if he/she is competent and qualified to perform the work, and that the person performing the work will be totally responsible to assure that all activities are carried out in a safe manner that will meet all applicable statutes. Resident(s) further guarantee that they will be accountable for any mishaps or accidents resulting from work done on the property, and that they will hold the Owner free from harm, litigation, or claims of any other person.

34. Radon:

Radon is a naturally occurring radioactive gas that may present health risks to persons who are exposed to it over time when it has accumulated in a building in sufficient quantities. Levels of radon gas that exceed federal and state guidelines have been found in buildings. Additional information regarding radon and radon testing may be obtained from your county public health office.

35. Lead-Based Paint:

Houses built before 1978 may contain lead-based paint. Lead from paint, paint chips, and dust can pose health hazards if not taken care of properly. Lead exposure is especially harmful to young children and pregnant women. Before renting pre-1978 housing, landlords must disclose the presence of known lead-based paint and lead-based paint hazards in the dwelling. Tenants must also receive a federally approved pamphlet about prevention of lead poisoning.

36. Smoke Detectors:

Smoke detectors have been installed in this residence. It is the tenant's responsibility to maintain the smoke detectors by testing them periodically and replacing batteries as recommended by the manufacturer. In the event that a detector is missing or inoperative, the tenant must notify the landlord immediately.

37. Default by Resident:

If any breach or violation of any provision of this contract by Resident occurs, or any information in Resident's application is found to be untrue or misleading, Owner or Owner's agent may terminate this contract, evict the Resident and take possession of the residence. In such a case, the Resident agrees to forfeit the Security Deposit, and Owner may still purse any remaining amounts due and owing.

38. Bankruptcy:

In the event of a bankruptcy or state insolvency proceeding being filed against the Resident(s), their heirs, or assigns, the Owner, his agent, heirs, or assigns, at their discretion, may immediately declare this contract null and void, and at once resume possession of the premises. No judicial officer shall ever have any rights, title, or interest in or to the above-described property by virtue of this agreement.

39. Renewal Term:

At the end of initial term herein, Owner may elect to renew for another term at an increase of 3% to 5% of current rental rate, depending on the market index.

40. Acknowledgment:

In this agreement, the singular number will also include the plural, the Masculine gender will include the Feminine, the term Owner will include Landlord, Lessor, and the term Resident will include Tenant, Lessee. The parties signing below acknowledge that they have read and understand all of the provisions of this agreement. This contract is bound by all heirs, executors, successors, and/or assigns.

41. Right To Sign:

The individual(s) signing this Lease/Rental Agreement as Resident(s) guarantee(s) that he/she/they have the right to sign for and to bind all occupants.

LEGAL CONTRACT: This is a legally binding contract. If you do not understand any part of this contract, seek competent legal advice before signing.

ACCEPTED THIS _____ day of _____20_____, at _____.

_____
Resident

_____
Resident

_____
Owner

NOTICE TO CHANGE RENT

Date: _____

To: _____

_____

THIS IS A NOTICE that the terms of the lease agreement under which you occupy the premises described above are about to be changed.

Beginning _____ (Month & Day), _____ (Year), your rent will be increased by _____ ($_____) per month from _____ ($_____) to _____ ($_____), payable in advance.

Owner/Manager

This notice was served by the Owner/Manager in the following manner (check those that apply):

____ by personal delivery to the tenant,
____ by leaving a copy with someone on the premises other than the tenant,
____ by mailing,
____ by posting.

HOUSE APPLICATION

NOTE: A $20 application fee, paid by cash or money order, must be paid before this application will be processed. NO personal checks will be accepted!

This application must be filled out and signed by all adults who will be living in the house.

All information will be carefully checked and verified. False information will result in automatic rejection of this application.

Please call our office if you have questions regarding this application.

This is an application for the house located at:

_____(Address)

FIRST APPLICANT:

Full Name (First, M.I., Last) _____

Date of Birth _____ Social Security No. _____

Phone (Day) (_____) _____ (Evening) (_____) _____

# of People Who Will Live in House _____

In Case of Emergency, Contact: _____

CURRENT ADDRESS: Own _____ Rent _____

Street _____Apt. No. _____

City _____ State _____ Zip _____

Number of years at this address _____

Name of owner _____

Phone number of owner (_____) _____

WHY ARE YOU MOVING? _____

_____

PREVIOUS ADDRESS: Own _____ Rent _____

Street _____ Apt. No. _____

City _____ State _____ Zip _____

Number of years at present address _____

Name of owner _____

Phone number of owner (_____) _____

WHY DID YOU MOVE? _____

_____

EMPLOYMENT INFORMATION:

Current Employer _____

Street _____ Phone (_____) _____

City _____ State _____ Zip _____

Title_____ Type of business _____

Number of years at this job _____ Self employed _____

Previous employer _____

Street _____ Phone (_____) _____

City _____ State _____ Zip _____

Title_____ Type of business _____

Number of years at this job _____ Self employed_____

CO-APPLICANT:

Full Name (First, M.I., Last) _____

Date of Birth _____ Social Security No. _____

Phone (Day) (_____) _____ (Evening) (_____) _____

# of People Who Will Live in House _____

In Case of Emergency Contact: _____

CURRENT ADDRESS: Own _____ Rent _____

Street _____ Apt. No. _____

City _____ State _____ Zip _____

Number of years at this address _____

Name of owner _____

Phone number of owner (_____) _____

WHY ARE YOU MOVING? _____

_____

PREVIOUS ADDRESS: Own _____ Rent _____

Street _____ Apt. No. _____

City _____ State _____ Zip _____

Number of years at present address _____

Name of owner _____

Phone number of owner (_____) _____

WHY DID YOU MOVE? _____

_____

EMPLOYMENT INFORMATION:

Current Employer _____

Street _____ Phone (_____) _____

City _____ State _____ Zip _____

Title_____ Type of business _____

Number of years at this job _____ Self-employed_____

Previous employer _____

Street _____ Phone (_____) _____

City _____ State _____ Zip _____

Title_____ Type of business _____

Number of years at this job _____ Self-employed_____

WEEKLY INCOME BEFORE TAXES:

	APPLICANT	CO-APPLICANT	TOTAL
Base Income			
Overtime			
Bonuses			
Other*			
Total Monthy Income			

DESCRIBE OTHER INCOME:

Applicant/Co-Applicant	Type	Amount
TOTAL		

*Alimony, child support, or separate maintenance income need not be revealed if the Applicant or Co-Applicant does not wish to have it considered as a basis for repaying this loan.

MONTHLY HOUSING EXPENSES:

	APPLICANT	CO-APPLICANT
Rent/House		
House/Renter's Insurance		
Utilities		
Other		
Total Monthly Payment		

APPLICANT AND CO-APPLICANT MUST BOTH ANSWER THESE QUESTIONS: ANSWER "YES" or "NO." If "Yes," please explain. Please call our office if you have any questions about this section.

Applicant: Yes/No

_____ Have you declared bankruptcy in the last 2 years?
_____ Have you ever been evicted or been asked to leave a property for any reason?
_____ Do you have any unpaid JUDGMENTS or COLLECTIONS?
_____ Have you ever been involved in a lawsuit as PLAINTIFF or DEFENDANT?
_____ Have you been convicted of a felony or misdemeanor in the last 5 years? (Except minor traffic violations)

_____ Have you ever had a home foreclosed on?

_____ Have you been pre-qualified to purchase a property by a bank or mortgage broker?

_____ Would you be willing to attend low-cost home buyer's classes?

_____ Do you intend to buy this home?

Please List Checking Account Numbers and Approximate Balances

Account Number   Approximate Balance

_____   \$ _____

_____   \$ _____

Please List Savings Account Numbers and Approximate Balances

Account Number   Approximate Balance

_____   \$ _____

_____   \$ _____

Please List All Types of Remodeling Work You Have Performed

Please list owner names and addresses of any major remodeling jobs you have completed

Owner's Name   Address of Remodeled Property   Type of Work Done

_____   _____   _____

_____   _____   _____

Co-Applicant: Yes/No

_____ Have you declared bankruptcy in the last 2 years?

_____ Have you ever been evicted or been asked to leave a property for any reason?

_____ Do you have any unpaid JUDGMENTS or COLLECTIONS?

_____ Have you ever been involved in a lawsuit as PLAINTIFF or DEFENDANT?

_____ Have you been convicted of a felony or misdemeanor in the last 5 years? (Except minor traffic violations)

_____ Have you ever had a home foreclosed on?

_____ Have you been pre-qualified to purchase a property by a bank or mortgage broker?

_____ Would you be willing to attend low-cost home buyer's classes?

_____ Do you intend to buy this home?

Please List Checking Account Numbers and Approximate Balances

Account Number   Approximate Balance

_____ $ _____

_____ $ _____

Please List Savings Account Numbers and Approximate Balances

Account Number   Approximate Balance

_____ $ _____

_____ $ _____

Please List All Types of Remodeling Work You Have Performed

Please list owner names and addresses of any major remodeling jobs you have completed

Owner's Name   Address of Remodeled Property   Type of Work Done

_____   _____   _____

_____   _____   _____

I certify under penalty of legal action that I have answered all of the above questions to the best of my ability. I give permission to _____ to use the provided information for purposes of verifying my qualifications to lease this property.

Applicant's Signature _____ Date _____

Co-Applicant's Signature _____ Date _____

CO-SIGNER AGREEMENT
(ADDENDUM TO RENTAL AGREEMENT)

Date: _____

Landlord: _____

Tenant: _____

This agreement is attached to and is hereby part of the Rental Agreement between the above-mentioned Landlord and Tenant, which is dated: _____.

My name is _____, and I have submitted a Rental Application in order to allow the Landlord to do a credit check on myself. I do not have any intention of residing in the unit referred to in the aforementioned Rental Agreement. I have read this Agreement and hereby promise to guarantee the Tenant's fulfillment of the financial commitment of this Agreement. I understand I will be required to pay for any unpaid rent, cleaning fees, and damages in the amount incurred by the Tenant under the Terms of this Agreement if, and only if, said Tenant(s) fail to pay.

_____   _____
Co-Signer Signature   Date

APPLICANT DISCLOSURE FORM

I hereby request that my application for the following rental property (address)_____be reviewed by _____.

Applicant Name: _____
Applicant Social Security Number: _____
Date of Birth: _____
Driver's License: _____State: _____
Applicant Address:_____
Applicant Home Phone: _____
Applicant Cell Phone: _____
Applicant Work Phone: _____
Address of Rental: _____

I give my authorization for _____to obtain and review my consumer credit report and any public records needed to come to an applicant decision. I also authorize _____to investigate any other personal information for the same purpose.

Signature_____

Date_____/_____/_____

APPLICANT DENIAL LETTER

Date: _____

Dear Applicant,

The application you placed for rental of the premises described as _____ located at _____ (street), _____ (city), ___ (state) _____ (zip) has unfortunately been denied.

The reason for our denial of your rental application was:

____1. Application contained incomplete or false information or the information that you provided on your application could not be verified.

____2. Previous rental history was reported as unfavorable for applicant.

____3. Did not meet income or debt qualifications.

____4. Information contained in your credit report.

In accordance to the Fair Credit Reporting Act, we are required to inform you where credit information was gathered from. We obtained this report from:

____1. Experian (TRW) Consumer Assistance, P. O. Box 949, Allen, TX 75002, 800-682-7654

____2. Trans Union Consumer Relations, P. O. Box 1000, 2 Baldwin Place, Chester, PA 19022, 800-888-4213

____3. CBI/Equifax Credit Information Service, P. O. Box 740241, Atlanta, GA 30374-2041, 800-685-1111

Insufficient credit information was obtained from the credit reporting agency marked above.

The credit reporting agency marked above was unable to provide a sufficient amount of information about you.

A person or company provided background information about you. Within 60 days of receiving this letter, you have the right to request information on the nature of the information provided. You must make this request in writing. Under federal law, we are prohibited from releasing information regarding the source of this information.

The credit reporting agency marked above may have gathered credit information on you based on reports from one of the other agencies. The agencies above serve only to provide credit information and were in no manner directly responsible for the denial of your rental application.

Under federal law, you have the right to receive a copy of your credit report, to dispute the accuracy and completeness of the report, and to insert a statement regarding specific entries on your credit report. Call the credit reporting agency marked above if you believe that there is inaccurate information contained on your credit report. You can also write the credit reporting agency at the address listed above to inform them of inaccuracies. A disclosure of the inaccuracies can be made orally, in writing, or electronically. Contact the agency marked above for specific details on filing complaints.

Within 60 days of ____/____/____, you are eligible to receive a free copy of your consumer credit report from the agency marked above.

You may have additional rights under the credit reporting or consumer protection laws of your state. If you wish, you may contact your state or local consumer protection agency or a state Attorney General's office.

Best Regards,

_____

Landlord/Property Manager

ASSIGNMENT OF RENTS FORM

Date:_____

Assignor(s): _____
Address: _____
City: _____ State: _____ Zip: _____
Assignee(s): _____
Address: _____
City: _____ State: _____ Zip: _____

Assignor, in consideration of $_____ and other valuable consideration tendered, the receipt of which has been acknowledged, hereby sells, assigns, transfers, and sets over to Assignee, his/her executors, and administrators, all the rents, issues, and profits now due and of which may become due under any lease, whether written or verbal, or any letting of, or any agreement for the use of or occupancy of any part of the premises described as _____

_____, which may have been or may be made or agreed to, or which may be made or agreed to by the Assignee under the power granted it. The purpose of this Agreement is to establish a total transfer and assignment of all such leases and agreements and all the avails under the leases and agreements to the Assignee and in particular those leases and agreements now on hand as follows:

Date of Lease	Lease Term	Monthly Rent
		$
		$

Rents will be paid monthly in advance on the aforementioned property.

SECURITY DEPOSIT AGREEMENT

Date of Acceptance:_____
Owner: _____
Tenant: _____

Owner hereby acknowledges receipt from the Tenant of $_____ for the Security against any default and/or damages for the unit Tenant is renting located at ___
_____.

This Deposit will be refunded to the Tenant in event that all conditions of the Lease Agreement are met upon the Tenant's departure.

_____
Owner

_____
Tenant

RENTAL PROPERTY KNOWLEDGE SHEET

Information on Rental Property

Address _____
Apt/Unit #_____ City/State _____ ZIP _____
Apt/Unit(s) Square Footage _____
Apt/Unit Mix: Studio _____ 1 Bedroom _____ 2 Bedroom/1 Bath ___
2 Bedroom/2 Bath _____

Rent: 1 Bedroom _____ 2 Bedroom/1 Bath _____ 2 Bedroom/2 Bath _____
Other _____
Application Fee _____ Security Deposit _____
Concessions _____
Rental Age _____ Construction Type _____Parking _____
Recreational Facilities _____ Laundry _____ Pets _____
Storage _____ Utilities (Who Pays?) _____
AC/Heat _____
Appliances _____
Floor coverings _____
Special Features/Comments _____

Community Information

School District _____ Elem. School _____
Middle School _____
High School _____ Jr. College _____
College _____
Trade School _____
Preschool(s) _____
Childcare _____
Places of Worship _____
Police/Fire Stations/Ambulance Service _____
Electric _____ Natural Gas _____ Telephone _____ Cable _____
Water _____ Sewer _____ Library _____
Post Office _____
Hospital/Pharmacies/Vet/Medical Facilities _____
Nearby Employment Centers _____
Transportation Availability _____
Groceries/Shopping _____
Local Services _____
Restaurants _____
Notes _____

Rental Market Information

Rental Competitors/Rental Rates/Concessions _____
_____
My Competitive Advantages _____
_____
My Competitive Disadvantages _____

WEEK-TO-WEEK RENTAL CONTRACT

This week-to-week rental contract is entered into on this date, _____, 20__ by and between _____(Owner) and _____(Renter).

WITNESSETH: That for and in consideration of the payment of the rent due and the performance of the covenants contained on the part of the Renter, said Owner does hereby demise and let unto the Renter, and Renter hires from Owner for use as a residence the specific premises hereby described as _____ ,which are located at _____ (street), _____ (city), ___ (state) _____ (zip) for a tenancy from week-to-week beginning on _____ (date) until _____ (ending date) at a weekly price of _____ dollars, for a total rental amount of _____(dollars), payable in advance on the first day of tenancy.

The following are also mutually agreed upon by both Renter and Owner:

1. Renter shall not violate any city ordinance or state law in or about the rental location.
2. Renter shall not sub-let the rental property, or any part thereof, or assign this contract without the written consent of said Owner.
3. Renter shall give immediate notice to the Owner or agent of same should any fire, theft, or vandalism occur on said premises.
4. Renter must not make any alterations or improvements to said property unless prior without written consent has been given by Owner.
5. If legal action takes place or must be initiated by Owner, Renter agrees to pay all costs, expenses, as well as all attorney's fees, as the court may affix.

Arrival Date: _____ Arrival Time: _____(__p.m./__a.m.)
Departure Date: _____ Departure Time: _____(__p.m./__a.m.)

Said premises __are / ___are not furnished with furniture, cooking utensils, kitchen equipment, linens, and bedding.

The following items are furnished: _____

_____

A non-refundable $_____ deposit is required in order to reserve said premises each week.

A deposit of $_____ for cleaning is required at time of check in. Cleaning deposit will be refunded only if said premises are left in clean condition at the time of check out.

If Owner is to incur any cleaning expenses in order to restore said premises to the condition they were in at the time of Renter's occupancy, the amount required for said restoration will be deducted from the cleaning deposit, and any remaining funds from the cleaning deposit will be refunded to the Renter.

_____

Owner Signed

_____

Owner Printed

_____

Renter Signed

_____

Renter Printed

TENANT WALK-THROUGH LIST

A walkthrough inspection of the property was completed on _____. The following items were inspected and their condition is noted with a yes if in working order and a no if it is not in working order:

- ❑ Stove
- ❑ Wall Oven
- ❑ Refrigerator
- ❑ Ice Maker
- ❑ Dishwasher
- ❑ Built-in Microwave
- ❑ Trash Compacter
- ❑ Disposer
- ❑ Freezer
- ❑ Window Fans
- ❑ Ceiling Fans
- ❑ Attic Fans
- ❑ Smoke Detectors
- ❑ Washer
- ❑ Dryer
- ❑ Electric Air Filter
- ❑ Central Vac
- ❑ Water Softener
- ❑ Exhaust Fans
- ❑ Alarm System
- ❑ Intercom

- ❏   Garage Door Openers
- ❏   Plumbing Fixtures
- ❏   Lighting Fixtures
- ❏   Window Treatments
- ❏   Storm Windows
- ❏   Storage Shed
- ❏   Wood Stove
- ❏   Fireplace
- ❏   Screen Doors
- ❏   Existing Screens
- ❏   Existing Storm Doors
- ❏   Heating and AC

Item that require repair/cleaning include:

1_____
2_____
3_____
4_____
5_____
6_____
7_____
8_____
9_____
10_____

Remarks: _____
_____

TENANT(S):

_____ / _____
Date   Signature

_____ / _____
Date   Signature

LANDLORD(S):

_____ / _____
Date   Signature

_____ / _____
Date   Signature

RENTAL MOVE IN/ MOVE OUT CHECKLIST

Date Move In: _____

Date Move Out: _____

Apartment/Unit #: _____

Tenant: _____

Condition of Room	Check In				Check Out				Comments
	New	Good	Okay	Poor	New	Good	Okay	Poor	
Entry/Halls									
Floors									
Walls									
Doorway									
Living Room									
Floors/Carpet									
Ceilings									
Walls									
Windows/Screens									
Ceiling Fan/Light Fixture									
Other: _____									
	New	Good	Okay	Poor	New	Good	Okay	Poor	
Kitchen									
Floors									
Ceilings									
Walls									
Light Fixtures									
Windows/Screens									

Condition of Room	Check In				Check Out				Comments
Cabinets									
Oven									
Refrigerator									
Dishwasher									
Sink									
Disposal									
Faucets									
Vents									
Counters									
Other: _____									
Dining Area									
Floors									
Ceilings									
Walls									
Light Fixtures									
Windows/ Screens									
Other: _____									
	New	Good	Okay	Poor	New	Good	Okay	Poor	
Bedroom #1									
Floors/Car-pets									
Ceilings									
Walls									
Light Fixtures									
Windows/ Screens									
Closet									
Other: _____									

Condition of Room	Check In				Check Out				Comments
Bedroom #2									
Floors/Carpets									
Ceilings									
Walls									
Light Fixtures									
Windows/Screens									
Closet									
Other: _____									

_____

Signed Landlord

_____

Signed Tenant

NOTICE OF CHANGE OF RENT

Date: _____ (month/day/year)

To: _____

_____

YOU ARE HEREBY NOTIFIED that the terms of your tenancy under which you reside in the aforementioned property are changing effective _____ (month) _____ (day) _____ (year).

As of said date, your rental amount will be increased by _____ dollars ($_____) per month from your current amount of _____ dollars ($_____) to the new amount of _____ dollars ($_____) per month, payable in advance.

_____   _____

Signed Owner/Manager   Date

This change of rent notice was served by the Owner/Manager by way of:

❑ personal delivery to said tenant   ❑ certified mail
❑ post on said tenant's door

DRUG-FREE HOUSING ADDENDUM

Date: _____
Tenant: _____
Landlord: _____
Rental Address: _____

In regard to the Rental Agreement made between the abovementioned Landlord and Tenant and the property listed above, the Parties hereby make agreement that the following addendum as of this date will hereby be in effect and part of the aforementioned Agreement.

With concern to a new Rental Agreement or renewal of a Rental Agreement and in regards to the aforementioned rental address, the Landlord and Tenant hereby agree to the following terms:

1. No person, whether the Tenant, a resident of the rental property, or a guest, shall in any way engage in any type of criminal activity, including any drug-related criminal behavior/activity, on or anywhere near the property. The abovementioned drug-related criminal activity includes the illegal manufacture, sale, distribution, use, or possession with intent to manufacture, sell, distribute, or use, of a controlled substance [as is defined in section 102 of the Controlled Substances Act (21 U.S.C.802)].

2. No person, whether the Tenant, a resident of the rental property, or a guest, shall engage in any type of activity or behavior that intends to assist in criminal activity, including anything drug-related.

3. Tenant and residents of the rental property are not permitted to engage in the manufacture, sale, or distribution of any illegal drugs at any location whether on or near the premises or otherwise.

4. No person, whether the Tenant, a resident of the rental property, or a guest, shall engage in any acts of violence or any threats of violence. These acts or threats of violence include, but are not limited to the unlawful possession or discharge of firearms on or near the property.

5. Tenant hereby agrees and understands that should any search warrants by issued by the court for this aforementioned rental address/property will cause an involuntary break of the Rental Agreement and the Landlord may request

eviction of the Tenant if that shall occur. Both Parties hereby understand that no arrests or convictions need to transpire prior to a breach of the Rental Agreement pursuant to this paragraph, just the judicial determination of probable cause to believe that some form of criminal and illegal activity has occurred will be deemed satisfactory for such breach.

_____

Tenant

_____

Landlord

ROOMMATE AGREEMENT (ADDENDUM TO THE RENTAL AGREEMENT)

Date: _____

This Agreement is made by and between

_____, _____,

_____, _____,

who have, on the _____ day of _____, 20____,

signed a lease for _____ (address) for a term lasting

from _____ to _____, a copy of which is attached to this agreement, and plan to reside on said premises; and wish to provide for the sharing of responsibilities as tenants of the rented premises.

ALL PARTIES AGREE:

1. That each of the parties will follow the rules and conditions set out in the attached lease.

   That each of the parties agrees to One _____(1/__) of the following expenses associated with the leased premises.* (This means one divided by the number of roommates. For example, in a household with 3 roommates, each member's share would be One-Third (1/3).)

   Check if applicable:
   _____ rent ($_____/mo.)
   _____ general maintenance and upkeep
   _____ gas
   _____ food
   _____ electricity
   _____ damages not due to the negligence identified party
   _____ telephone service

_____ water

_____ other _____

If any of the parties pays more than the One _____ (1/__) share, the other parties agree to reimburse the first party.

2. Each party agrees to pay for any long-distance telephone calls he or she makes.

3. A security or damage deposit in the amount of $_____ will be paid to Owner/agent. The parties agree that the total deposit is $_____ and that each tenant's portion is $_____. Unless otherwise stated in the lease, the tenants agree that the landlord will be asked to return the deposit in the following manner:

    _____

    _____.

    If one roommate subleases their room to a new tenant, unless otherwise stipulated in the lease, the security deposit exchange shall be conducted in the following way:

    _____

    _____

4. Each of the parties agrees to pay his/her share of the rent, utilities, and phone in a timely manner during the entire term of the lease unless those responsibilities are taken over by a subtenant.

5. A roommate may sublease his/her room to a new tenant if the following conditions are met:
    a. the party arranges to sublet his/her share to a subtenant at his/her expense.
    b. the subtenant is acceptable to the remaining parties, who will not unreasonably withhold their acceptance.
    c. the owner/manager gives written consent to the subtenant.

6. That repairs or improvements to the premises, the costs of which are to be shared by the parties, exceeding $ _____ shall be approved in advance.

7. If pets are permitted under the lease, each pet owner shall be solely responsible for all damages caused by his or her pet, including, but not limited to, damage to furniture, carpeting, doors, lawn, and garden.

8. Additional provisions (rules for music, smoking, housecleaning, etc.):

    _____

    _____

Signature of Each Roommate:

_____   _____

_____   _____

(Each roommate should be given a copy for their records and a copy should be given to the landlord).

WATERBED AGREEMENT
(ADDENDUM TO THE RENTAL AGREEMENT)

Date	Rental Address
Management/Owner	Renter

This agreement is part of the Rental Agreement dated _____
between Management/Owner and Renter for the above-mentioned residential unit. The
Renter desires to keep a waterbed described as _____
___ in the unit occupied under the Rental Agreement, and because the Rental Agreement
expressly prohibits waterbeds within the premises without written permission from the
Management, Renter hereby agrees to:

1.   Keep only one (1) waterbed approved by Management for the unit. Waterbed
     shall consist of _____.

2.   Consult with Management about the location of the waterbed on the prem-
     ises. Renter agrees to employ a qualified professional to install and dismantle
     the bed according to the manufacturer's specifications and also agrees not to
     relocate it without the consent of Management.

3.   Allow Management to inspect the waterbed installation at any and all reason-
     able times and to remedy any problems or potential problems right away.

4.   Provide Management with a copy of a valid liability insurance policy in the
     amount of $_____ , naming Owner as the insured, which will cover the
     waterbed installation, and to renew the policy as required for uninterrupted
     coverage.

5.   Immediately cover the cost for any damage caused by the waterbed and, in
     addition, to add $ _____ to the security/cleaning depos-
     it, any of which may be used for cleaning, repairs, or delinquent rent when
     Renter vacates. Within _____ days after Renter proves to
     Management that the waterbed is no longer to be found on the property,
     waterbed damages will be assessed and remainder of this extra deposit will be
     returned to Resident.

6.   Cover the additional time, effort, costs, and risks involved in said waterbed
     installation with payment of additional rent of $ _____, which
     [ ] includes [ ] does not include the premium for the waterbed liability insur-
     ance policy described in item 4.

7.   Management reserves the right to retract this permission to keep a waterbed should the Renter violate this agreement.

_____

Signed Management/Owner

_____

Signed Renter

SMOKE DETECTOR RENTAL AGREEMENT ADDENDUM

Date: _____

Tenant: _____

Landlord: _____

Rental Address: _____

Landlord hereby certifies that all smoke detectors set up in the above listed rental property are all in operating condition at the time of Tenant's move in. Smoke detectors in this unit are located in the following places:

1. _____

2. _____

3. _____

4. _____

As the Tenant you hereby agree that the smoke detectors are in operating condition. I also understand that to keep them in working condition, I will need to check and replace the batteries to each device on an as-needed basis. Replacement batteries are the Tenant's responsibilities. Each detector should be tested once a month to be sure they are in working order. If any problem arises with one or more of the smoke detectors once the monthly battery check and device test occurs, it is your responsibility to immediately notify the Landlord to guarantee these units offer the early discovery of a fire or smoke should such occur. We request serious teamwork between the Tenant and Landlord with this issue.

_____

Tenant

_____

Landlord

UTILITY ADDENDUM FOR RENTAL AGREEMENT

Date: _____

Tenant: _____

Landlord: _____

Rental Address: _____

This addendum is hereby made to the Rental Agreement made between the aforementioned Tenant and Landlord for the property listed above.

The Landlord hereby agrees to provide the water and sewer services for the rental property. Tenant's payment for service shall be made in one of the following manners:

1.   Landlord will hold the billing for the utility service and Tenant will make a set utility payment of $_____ per month with his/her rent. This amount will be applied to the water and sewer bill.

2.   Tenant will pay amount of utility bill as provided by the Landlord each quarter. This amount is due on the 1st of the month that the bill is due. Payment may be made with the rent due. Amount owed will be provided by the Landlord by the 15th of the previous month.

The Tenant and Landlord may together review the water meter at the beginning and end of the Rental Agreement period in order to pro-rate the utility fee for those months.

_____

Tenant

_____

Landlord

UTILITIES GUARANTEE LETTER

Date: _____

Landlord: _____

Property Address: _____

To Whom It May Concern:

The Landlord listed above has my permission to change all utilities, water, and cable into Tenant's name for the abovementioned property. Tenant hereby agrees to pay all bills that come from the use of those utilities at the property during the dates of tenancy corresponding with those agreed to in the Rental Agreement: _____ (start date) to _____ (end date).

Tenant 1 Name:	Tenant 2 Name:
Social Security #:	Social Security #:

_____

Tenant 1 Signed

_____

Tenant 2 Signed

NOTIFICATION OF INTENT TO VACATE RENTAL PROPERTY

Rental Address: _____

Name on Lease: _____

Vacate Date: _____

Lease Expiration Date: _____

Forwarding Address: _____

Lessee Signature(s):

Name_____Date_____

Name_____Date_____

As per the lease agreement, it is the lessee's responsibility to leave the premises clean and in good condition. All personal property is to be removed by the date indicated above. Any refund of security deposit funds will be sent to the forwarding address as stated above, as prescribed by law.

ACKNOWLEDGMENT LETTER OF NOTICE OF INTENT TO VACATE

Date: _____

Dear Tenant:

This letter is sent to you in acknowledgment that we have received your Notice of Intent to Vacate the premises that lists your plan to move out of the premises on _____ (date).

Please be aware that this is to be a firm date and may only be changed by written consent between both the Lessee and Lessor. If you have satisfied the terms and conditions of your Lease/Rental Agreement you may expect a refund of your deposit. Please keep in mind that a complete refund of your deposit will be determined based on whether you have completed the following list:

1. Your unit must be returned in good, clean condition, including removal of all belongings and trash, and special cleaning attention to appliances and bathrooms.

2. Return all keys. Be sure all unit, mail, and laundry keys are returned to management within _____ days of vacating the premises. You will be responsible for all rent until you return all keys.

3. Be sure all final utility bills are paid in full and services have been transferred from your name.

4. Your last month's rent should be paid in full. Your security deposit may NOT be used for this purpose. The deposit will be returned via check after final inspection and unit review has occurred.

5. Leave your forwarding address with the Landlord for any mail or unit issues.

6. Landlord will not be responsible for any items you leave in the unit after you have returned your keys (examples include telephones, clothing, cable boxes, satellite dishes, etc).

Keep in mind your liability will not be limited by the amount of your security deposit. Should charges and fees be over the amount of your deposit be required, you will be charged for these additional amounts.

We hope your tenancy with us has been a pleasant one. Please contact us with any questions or concerns you have. Thank you.

Sincerely,

_____

Landlord

RENTER EXIT INTERVIEW

Please provide the following feedback so that we may ensure the highest quality service to our lessees.

Reason for vacating: _____

Would you say that your rental unit was:

Excellent   Good   Fair   Poor   Very Poor

Please list improvements that could be made to your unit:

_____

_____

Comments: _____

_____

Date:_____

Reviewed By:_____

RECEIPT OF RENTAL PAYMENT

Date: _____

Tenant Name: _____

Address: _____

Dear Tenant,

Your payment of $_____ was received from _____ on _____ (date). This payment is for the rent from _____ to _____ for the property address listed above.

Thank you,

_____

Landlord

REJECTION LETTER

Date: _____

Applicant Name: _____

Applicant Address: _____

_____

Rental Address: _____

_____

Dear Applicant,

We have received your application for tenancy. Unfortunately, we have to inform you that your application has been denied for the rental property listed above. The reason for this denial of your application is:

❏   Prior residency information provided was not able to be verified.

❏   Job history provided was insufficient.

❏   Poor or no credit history.

❏   Income not enough to meet rental requirements.

0Due to the denial of your application in part based on your credit history, the Fair Credit Reporting Act requires the following disclosures be made to you:

The credit agency we received your information from was:

_____

_____

0The credit reporting company did not make the decision to take the adverse action and is unable to provide you with the specific reasons why the adverse action was taken. Under Section 612 of the Fair Credit Reporting Act, you have the right to receive a free copy of your credit report(s) from the reporting agency within 60 days. You have the right to dispute with the credit reporting agency the accuracy or completeness of the credit report.

0Should you have any other questions regarding your application or this letter, please do not hesitate to contact us during normal business hours.

Regards,

_____

Landlord/Owner

Landlord Forms

PET AGREEMENT

Date: _____

This agreement is attached to and forms a part of the _____ Agreement dated _____ , between _____ , Management, and _____ , Tenant, for the residential unit located at _____ .

Resident desires to keep a pet/pets named _____ and described as _____ in the dwelling Tenant occupies under the Lease Agreement referred to above. This agreement specifically prohibits keeping pets without Management's permission, so the Tenant hereby agrees to:

1. Keep his/her pet under control during entire term of tenancy.
2. Never leave his/her pet unattended for unreasonable lengths of time.
3. Keep his/her pet restrained, not tethered, when outside Tenant's dwelling at any place on the property.
4. Properly and swiftly dispose of his/her pet's feces and waste.
5. Never leave any type of food or water for pet, or any other animal, outside the unit.
6. Keep his/her pet from causing any irritation or distress to other tenants, visitors, or management and quickly remedy any complaints made to the Management.

7. Remove all of his/her pet's offspring from the property within eight weeks of birth.

8. Pay immediately for any damage, loss, or expense caused by his/her pet and, add $ _____ to the security/cleaning deposit, any of which may be used for cleaning, repairs, or late rent when Tenant vacates the unit. Within _____ days after Tenant proves said pet is no longer kept on the premises, this added deposit minus any assessed pet damages will be returned to Tenant.

9. Management reserves the right to revoke permission to keep the pet should Tenant violate this agreement.

_____

Signed   Management

_____

Signed   Tenant

TENANT'S SUBORDINATION AGREEMENT

Date: _____

_____ (Tenant/Lessee), a corporation authorized to transact business within the State of _____, enters into this Agreement to subordinate all rights in and to its leasehold interest in the Lease, dated _____, signed by _____(Lessor)

Address: _____

City: _____ State: _____ Zip: _____

and

_____ (Tenant/Lessee)

Address: _____

City: _____ State: _____ Zip: _____

a) This Lease (hereafter referred to as "Lease") was assigned to _____ _____ on or about _____ (Date) to the

Mortgage Deed and Note given by _____(Lessor) in favor of _____, its successors and/or assigns ("_____ _____"), to any renewal, extension, modification, or consolidation of such mortgage.

b) _____ (Lessor)

represents to _____ that _____ (Tenant/Lessee) is current with all rents due under the LEASE, as set forth in an Estoppel Certificate executed by _____ _____ contemporaneously with this Agreement, and that the subordination set forth in this Agreement shall be without counterclaims, defense, or offset.

_____

(Signature)

LESSOR: _____
(Signature)

TENANT/LESSEE: _____
(Signature)

STATE OF _____, COUNTY OF _____

The foregoing instrument was acknowledged before me, this _____ day of _____, 20 _____.

_____ Notary Public

(SEAL) State of _____

My Commission Expires: _____

PROBLEM TENANT REPORT FORM

Landlord, please fill out this form for every violation/disturbance and place in tenant's file.* After _____ forms are placed in file, please send a warning to the tenant. If additional reports are filed, please consider the eviction process.

Date:	Tenant Name:	Tenant's Address/ Unit Number:	Violation/Disturbance Information

Landlord, please note that a violation may include property damage, late rent payments, poor property maintenance, and/or high noise complaints.

TENANT/PROPERTY INCIDENT REPORT

Date of the incident: _____ 20_____

Time of the incident: _____ a.m./p.m.

Location of the incident: _____

Apt. #: _____

Who was involved? _____

_____

What happened? _____

_____

Any witnesses? If yes, who? _____

_____

Where do they live? _____

_____

Insurance adjuster contacted? _____

Fire department contacted? _____

Police department contacted? _____

Action or follow up? _____

_____

Who prepared this report? _____

cc: Tenant file

Attorney

Insurance company

Section 8 leasing officer (if applicable)

30-DAY NOTICE TO TERMINATE TENANCY

To (Tenant Name)	Date
(and all occupying parties)	
Address Of Premises	

This is a notice that you are required to move from and remove all of your possessions from the aforementioned premises within thirty (30) days.

The purpose of this notice is to hereby terminate the Lease/Rental Agreement for the unit of which is described above. Failure to comply will result in legal action to ensue against you to recover possession of said property, to officially declare the Lease/Rental Agreement as terminated, and recover any rent due or fees for any damages incurred during the unlawful tenancy period.

You are hereby also advised that any rent on the above-mentioned property is due and payable up to and including the date of termination of your tenancy under this notice.

_____

Owner/Management Agent

_____

Served By

CHART OF FEES TENANT MAY BE CHARGED AFTER INSPECTION UPON LEASE TERMINATION

If tenant does not return the residence in the same condition as when tenant began renting, the following chart describes the minimum charges which will be deducted from the Security Deposit tenant paid upon signing of lease. Any cost related to cleaning, labor, repairs, removals, trash pickup, replacements, where applicable will be deducted. Any rent income loss due to the time it takes to make repairs or any of the above mentioned items, will also be deducted from the security deposit.

Minimum Charge List	
Charges for Cleaning Not Done by Tenant:	
Stove/Oven	$
Refrigerator	$
Kitchen Sink	$
Cabinets	$
Counter tops	$
Bathroom Toilet	$
Bathroom Shower/Tub	$
Medicine Cabinet	$
Bathroom Sink Area	$
Windows	$
Closet Areas	$
Charges for Floorings Not Cleaned by Tenant:	
Tile	$
Carpet	$
Kitchen Floors	$
Bathroom Floors	$
Bedroom Floors	$
Other: _____	$
Charges for Trash Removal:	
On Property	$
Per Room	$
For Removal of Large Trash	$
Extensive Cleaning Charges:	
Per Hour Amount	$
Charges for Damages:	

Minimum Charge List	
For damages to walls due to negligence (per room)	$
For removing of tenant's wall coverings (per hour fee)	$
Covering of nail holes/ other small holes (per hole fee)	$
Covering/Fixing Large Holes (per hole fee)	$
Cigarette Burns (per burn fee)	$
Carpet/Rug/Tile Replacement	$
Light Bulbs (per bulb fee)	$
Unreturned Key Fee (per key fee)	$
Lock Replacement (per replacement)	$
Lawn Maintenance (min. fee)	$
Screen Replacement (per screen fee)	$
Window Replacement (per pane)	$

Resident hereby agrees that besides any fees owed for these issues listed above, the deposit will be returned within _____ days after date set with Management for final vacancy.

Resident understands that any amount listed above is for the minimum cleaning and damage repair.

Tenant Signed _____

Owner/Manager Signed _____

NOTICE OF INTENT TO ENTER

Date:	Renter Name and Unit Address:

This notice is to inform you that on or about _____ ❑ a.m./ ❑ p.m. on _____ (month/day/year), the Owner, Manager, Owner's agent, or Owner's employees intend to enter the premises mentioned above which you rent and occupy. They will need to stay approximately _____ ❑ minutes/ ❑ hours.

The reason for entering the property is:

_____

_____

You are not required to be present to provide access to the unit. The party who is entering will first knock and, after determining that no one is available to answer, will enter using a passkey.

This notice is intended to notify you at least twenty-four (24) hours in advance.

This notice was personally delivered by the Owner/Manager at the following time:
_____ ❑ a.m./ ❑ p.m. on _____ (month/day/year).

_____

Owner/Manager

NOTICE OF INTENT TO ENTER VERSION 2

Dear (_____):

This is a notification that the landlord, or a representative of the Landlord, will be entering your premises on (date) _____ at (approximate time) in order to:

_____ Make the following repairs: _____

_____ Show the unit to:
_____ Prospective renters
_____ Contractors

_____ Other: _____

You have the right to be present during this time. Please notify the landlord immediately if the date or time is problematic. You are, of course, welcome to be present. If you have any questions or if the date/time is problematic, please notify the Landlord at (___-___-____).

Landlord Signature:_____Date:_____

APARTMENT/UNIT SERVICE CALL

Date:	
Renter:	Unit/Apartment #:

Hello. Your apartment/unit was serviced today. The following occurred:

❑ Filter Changed Today
❑ Heat Checked Today
❑ Air Conditioning Checked Today
❑ _____ Checked Today
❑ _____ Checked Today
❑ _____ Checked Today

Please be aware that the following items were not completed:

1. _____
2. _____
3. _____

If you have any questions or require additional assistance, please contact Management.

Service Call Completed By: _____

TENANT EMERGENCY/SERVICE CALL INFORMATION

NEW TENANT INFORMATION

Dear Tenant:

Welcome! This list contains the numbers that you may need to contact for emergency services or service calls while a resident at your new address. During an emergency, you may find you are unable to reach the owner or myself. In this situation, please be sure to contact one of the numbers below for your need to be addressed after office hours. Please let us know if you have any questions. We will be sure to send you updates to any of these numbers should a change occur.

Thank you,

_____

Landlord Signature

In Case Of:	Who to Call/ Action to Take:	Phone Number:
Fire		
Criminal Activity		
Ambulance/Paramedic Assistance Needed		
Water Line Break	Turn off Water Valve	----------------
Gas Leak		
Electricity Outage (Except for billing issues)		
Emergency Repair Necessary		
Utility Companies:	**Who:**	**Phone Number:**
Phone		
Electric		
Water		
Cable		
Closest Community:	**Name:**	**Phone Number:**
School		
Shopping Center		
Pharmacy (24-Hours)		
Laundry		
Furniture and Appliance Rental/Purchase Store		
Library		
Bank		

Post Office		
Public Transportation (Bus, Cab, Trolley, etc)		
Newspaper		
Other:	**Name:**	**Phone Number:**
_____		
_____		

CRIME REPORT REQUEST

Use this form to request a crime report on an address from your local police department.

Date:	From:

Dear Officer,

I am hereby requesting a crime report and a "call to service" report for the below property address:

_____

_____

I would appreciate this request be handled in a timely manner and greatly appreciate your assistance. Please send this report to my attention at the following location:

_____

_____

You may contact me at (_____) _____-_____. Thank you for your assistance,

_____

Landlord Signature

REFUSAL TO RENT/LEASE FORM

Date: _____

Dear Applicant,

Your request to rent or lease property located at the following address _____
_____ has been denied. The reason for this denial is specified below.

- ❏ Your application was incomplete.
- ❏ You have insufficient credit references.
- ❏ We were unable to verify the credit references provided.
- ❏ We were unable to verify credit as no credit file available.
- ❏ Your credit file is insufficient.
- ❏ Your credit file shows delinquent accounts.
- ❏ Your credit file shows too many obligations.
- ❏ Your past rental history has been too short.

❑ We were unable to verify your current residence.
❑ We were unable to verify your employment.
❑ Your employment record has been irregular or temporary.
❑ Your employment record shows too short a time period of current employment.
❑ Your income is insufficient to handle the rent/lease amount.
❑ We were unable to verify your income.
❑ Your credit file shows bankruptcy.
❑ Your credit history shows you have been evicted from a previous residence(s).
❑ Your credit file shows you have been involved in a suit, garnishment of wages, foreclosure, or repossession.
❑ Other: _____

Due to the reason(s) marked above, we are unable to provide you tenancy. We do not rent/lease to anyone based on these issues.

Thank you,

_____
Management/Owner

We obtained information from: _____

Fair Credit Reporting Act
Under the Fair Credit Reporting Act, you have the right to make a written request, within 60 days of receipt of this notice, for disclosure of the nature of the adverse information. The Federal Equal Credit Opportunity Act prohibits creditors from discriminating against credit applicants on the basis of race, color, religion, national origin, sex, marital status, age (provided the applicant has the capacity to enter into a binding contract), because all or part of the applicant's income derives from any public assistance program or because the applicant has in good faith exercised any right under the Consumer Credit Protection Act. The Federal agency that administers compliance with this law concerning this creditor is the Federal Trade Commission, Equal Credit Opportunity, Washington, D.C. 20580.

INSPECTION FAILURE LETTER

Date: _____

To: _____

_____

Dear Tenant:

During the inspection of your unit which took place on _____ (date), the following conditions were found to be lower than the standards required by your Rental/Lease Agreement. You are hereby notified that you have _____ days from the date of this letter to correct these conditions to the standards set in your agreement. We will also be submitting your residence to a weekly inspection for the next _____ months while we verify that the conditions are remaining in the right standards. If neglect continues, we will have no choice but to take action as specified under your Rental/Lease Agreement.

(Landlord, please fill in the precise problem in the space provided by each main problem.)

- ❑ Lawn Care Issues: _____.
- ❑ Trees/Bushes Issues: _____.
- ❑ Animal Dropping Issues: _____.
- ❑ Broken Windows/Screens/Doors/Gates: _____.
- ❑ Trash Removal/Pick Up: _____.
- ❑ Walls/Doors: _____.
- ❑ Paint Touch Up: _____.
- ❑ Leak Repair: _____.
- ❑ Loose Hardware Tightened or Replaced: _____.
- ❑ Filters/Pads Replaced: _____.
- ❑ Broken-down Vehicle Removal: _____.
- ❑ Other: _____.

Please address these areas of concern as soon as possible. Thank you.

Sincerely,

_____

Landlord/Owner

Late Payment Forms

FIRST NOTICE: LATE RENT

Date: _____

Resident(s) include:

Resident Adult 1: _____
Resident Adult 2: _____
Resident Child(ren): _____

Rental Residence Address:

_____

Dear _____,

This is a friendly reminder that we have yet to receive your rent payment for the month of _____. We ask that you please remit by _____ (date). Payment made by this date will ensure no late penalties are assessed.

Thank you for your prompt attention to this matter.

Respectfully,

_____

Landlord Signature

_____

Landlord Printed

Should you have any questions regarding this matter, please call _____.

NOTICE OF OVERDUE RENT

Date: _____

TO: (Tenant's Name & Address)

_____

_____

FROM: (Landlord's Name & Address)

_____

_____

Your rent in the amount of $_____ was due on _____ (date) for the month of _____ in which you were occupying the premises located at _____. We ask that you please bring your payment to the landlord's address as given above or call us immediately at _____.

If you have already remitted payment, please disregard this notice.

Thank you,

_____

Landlord Signature

NOTICE OF PAST DUE RENT

TO BE SENT VIA CERTIFIED MAIL

Date _____

Resident(s) include:

Resident Adult 1: _____
Resident Adult 2: _____
Resident Child(ren): _____

Rental Residence Address:

_____

Rent Due Date: _____
Rent Amount: $ _____
Rent Amount Past Due $ _____
Late Charge Amount $ _____
Total Rent Amount Due $ _____
Estimated Amount of Potential Court Fees $_____

According to the records of _____, you are behind in your rent. We are unable to keep our rental properties maintained (including the mortgage, utilities, and taxes) if we do not receive the rental payments due to us in a timely manner. While we hope that your delinquency period is just an oversight, we will have to impose a past due rental notice and late charge. This letter hereby serves as that notice.

We are giving you three (3) days to pay this past due amount and additional late charge. Many times our tenants fail to pay the rent due to financial issues and as much as we understand and sympathize with the predicament, we cannot provide free housing without getting ourselves into financial difficulties. If you find you are unable to pay the amount past due and late charges, we do require that you move. If, after this three (3) day grace period, you have yet to pay the amount due or have not vacated the home, we will file for a court order to have your possessions removed from the premises. If this situation comes to a court suit, this will require you to pay not only the total amount due from past rent and late charges, but will also require you pay all court costs associated with this suit.

It is in the best interest of the tenant to pay the amount due before a court action is taken. This action could affect not only your credit rating, but also your attempt to rent another property. If you move out of the residence without first paying all rent and charges due, the court will grant a judgment against you that could result in the garnishment of your income or the seizing of your possessions.

PAYMENT ARRANGEMENT

I am currently renting (address) _____ from (owner) _____. I acknowledge that I currently owe $_____ in past-due rent.

I promise that I will pay the above amount owed, in full, by the date of _____, 20____.

In the event that I do not follow through with the above promise for any reason, I shall vacate said premises immediately by the above mentioned date. If I fail to do so, I give my permission to owner to change the locks and allow the owner to re-rent said premises. If said premises are unfurnished, I give said owner or agent permission to remove the furniture from said premises and set it out on the street. The owner will return all personal clothing and belongings to me.

I realize it is my responsibility to pick up my personal belongings and articles no later than 48 hours after owner has changed the locks.

Date: _____ 20_____.

_____

Signed Management

_____

Signed Resident

NOTICE TO VACATE PREMISES

The following notice will be considered VOID if rent due and all charges are paid within the time limit provided.

To _____ (Tenant) and everyone residing at said premises. You are hereby notified that _____ (Landlord) wants you to vacate the premises you are currently occupying and in which you have been renting from me (us). Premises is situated in _____ (County) and State of _____ and is described as follows: _____

Grounds: _____

Your compliance with this notice on or before the _____ (day) of _____ (month) in the year _____ will prevent any court action to be taken by me as stated previously.

YOU ARE BEING ASKED TO LEAVE THE PREMISES. IF YOU DO NOT LEAVE, AN EVICTION ACTION MAY BE INITIATED AGAINST YOU. IF YOU ARE IN DOUBT REGARDING YOUR LEGAL RIGHTS AND OBLIGATIONS AS A TENANT, IT IS RECOMMENDED THAT YOU SEEK LEGAL ASSISTANCE.

Respectfully,

_____

Landlord Printed

_____

Landlord Signed

_____

Date

_____

Address

Should you have any questions regarding this matter, please call _____.

PAST DUE LAND CONTRACT PAYMENT

Date: _____

Tenant: _____

Address: _____

City State Zip: _____

Dear _____:

As of today's date, we have not received your payment for the month of _____.
You now owe $_____ in rent, plus a $ _____ late charge. This payment is due
immediately if you wish to continue living in the house.

This is the 30-day notice of default required in Paragraph _____ of your Land Contract.
This paragraph states in part:

(Insert text of YOUR land contract's default payment paragraph here)

You will note that unless you correct the default by paying the money owed, the entire balance will immediately become due, and you will immediately owe the entire price of the
house. If you move out on or before _____ (30 days from today),
leave the house in a clean and orderly condition, and return the keys to me, I will sue you
only for the unpaid back rent.

You have three options:

1. Make a full payment of unpaid rent and late charges and continue buying the
    house under the land contract.
2. Move out immediately, leaving the property clean and ready to rent. You will
    owe only the payments for the time you are in the house.
3. Wait for the court to evict you and issue a judgment for the entire amount due
    on the land contract.

I sincerely regret that you were unable to keep up your payments. If you have questions,
feel free to give me a call.

Sincerely,

_____

Contract Holder

SECOND NOTICE: LATE RENT

Date: _____

Resident(s) include:

Resident Adult 1: _____

Resident Adult 2: _____

Resident Child(ren): _____

Rental Residence Address:

_____

Dear _____,

This is a reminder that we have yet to receive your rent payment for the month of _____. We ask that you please remit by _____ (date). According to the Lease Agreement signed by you, the rent for this property is due on the _____ of every month with a late fee to be assessed after the _____ day of every month if said rent payment has not been made.

Therefore, per said Lease Agreement, we are placing a late charge on your account in the amount of $_____. We ask that you include this late fee when providing rent payment. We ask that you please remit rent and late fee payment immediately to avoid further action.

Thank you for your prompt attention to this matter.

Respectfully,

_____

Landlord Signature

_____

Landlord Printed

Should you have any questions regarding this manner, please call _____.

Appendix D

Lead Paint Forms

LEAD DISCLOSURE RULES SUMMARY

Adapted from
www.epa.gov/Compliance/resources/policies/civil/tsca/lead.pdf
Please check with an attorney for the correct format and procedure for your state.

Summary of Rule and Requirement

The purpose of the Disclosure Rule is to ensure that individuals and families receive the information necessary to protect themselves and their families from lead-based paint and/or lead based paint hazards. This information will help families and individuals make informed housing decisions to reduce their risk of exposure to lead hazards.

The Disclosure Rule requires that sellers, lessors, and agents must comply with certain requirements when selling or leasing target housing. For purposes of the Disclosure Rule, "Seller" is defined as any entity that transfers legal title to target housing, in whole or in part. The Disclosure Rule defines "Lessor" as any entity that offers target housing for lease, rent, or sublease. "Purchaser" is defined as an entity that enters into an agreement to purchase an interest in target housing under the Disclosure Rule. "Lessee" is defined as any entity that enters into an agreement to lease, rent, or sublease target housing. Finally, the Disclosure Rule defines "Agent" as any party who enters into a contract with a seller or lessor, including any person who enters into a contract with a representative of the Lessor or Seller, to sell or lease target housing.

The Disclosure Rule requires that before a Purchaser or Lessee is obligated under any contract to purchase or lease target housing, certain requirements must be met. These requirements include the following:

- Sellers and Lessors must disclose the presence of any known lead-based paint and/or lead-based paint hazards to the Purchasers and Lessees and to any Agent;
- Sellers and Lessors must provide Purchasers and Lessees with any available records or reports pertaining to the presence of lead-based paint and/or lead-based paint hazards in the target housing;
- Sellers and Lessors must provide Purchasers and Lessees with an EPA-approved lead hazard information pamphlet;
- Sellers must grant Purchasers a 10-day period to conduct a risk assessment or inspection for the presence of lead-based paint and/or lead-based paint hazards;
- Sellers and Lessors must complete a Disclosure Form certifying compliance with the Disclosure requirements;
- Sellers and Lessors must retain a copy of the Disclosure Form for at least three years from completion of the transaction; and
- Each Agent involved in any transaction to lease or sell target housing must ensure compliance with all requirements of the Disclosure Rule.

The Disclosure Rule contains exclusions for the following transactions:

- Sales of target housing at foreclosure;
- Leases of target housing that have been found to be lead-based paint free by the appropriate inspector;
- Short term leases of 100 days or less;
- Lease renewals where previous disclosure has occurred;
- The purchase, sale or servicing of mortgages;
- The sale or lease of 0-bedroom dwellings; and
- Housing for the elderly or persons with disabilities (unless any child under six (6) years of age resides or is expected to reside in such target housing).

I. Consultation with EPA Headquarters

In the implementation of this enforcement program, EPA Headquarters is requiring that EPA Regional Lead Coordinators ("Regions") consult with Headquarters on a specified number of enforcement actions to ensure consistency and to address any unique issues. Therefore, each region must receive concurrence from Headquarters on the initial six (6) civil administrative complaints and notices of noncompliance before issuance. The Regions must also contact and consult with EPA Headquarters on the use of TSCA subpoenas to enforce the Disclosure Rule. These consultation and concurrence efforts will help ensure national consistency and address issues that arise during implementation of the Disclosure Rule enforcement program.

II. Enforcement Response Policy Applicability

This Disclosure Rule Enforcement Response Policy is immediately applicable and will be used to determine the enforcement response and to calculate penalties in administrative enforcement actions concerning violations of the Disclosure Rule.

III. Applicability to Federal Facilities

As discussed in Section III below, the Disclosure Rule defines "Seller" and "Lessor" to include government agencies. Thus, when a Federal facility or government agency is the Seller or Lessor of target housing as defined in the statute and the rule, the requirements of Section 1018 and the Disclosure Rule apply to such facility or agency.

Section 1018(b)(5) makes a violation of the Disclosure Rule a prohibited act under Section 409 of TSCA and the facility or agency is then subject to EPA enforcement authority under Section 16 of TSCA. Section 408 of TSCA subjects each department, agency, and instrumentality of the executive, legislative, and judicial branches of the Federal Government to all Federal, State, interstate, and local requirements, both substantive and procedural, respecting lead-based paint, lead-based paint activities, and lead-based paint hazards. The Federal, State, interstate, and local substantive and procedural requirements referred to in Section 408 of TSCA include, but are not limited to, all administrative orders and all civil and administrative penalties and fines regardless of whether such penalties or fines are punitive or coercive in nature. The Disclosure Rule contains Federal requirements respecting lead-based paint, lead-based paint activities, and lead-based paint hazards. Therefore, Federal facilities are subject to the Disclosure Rule requirements.

EPA thus has express penalty authority over Federal facilities. In assessing penalties against Federal agencies, EPA will apply the Disclosure Rule Enforcement Response Policy. Before a penalty order becomes final, Section 16(a)(2) of TSCA requires the Administrator to provide the Federal agency with notice and an opportunity for a formal hearing on the record in accordance with the Administrative Procedures Act. 40 C.F.R. Part 22, sets forth the U.S. Environmental Protection Agency's (EPA's) general rules of administrative practice governing the assessment of administrative penalties. The Consolidated Rules of Practice also require that before a final order of the Environmental Appeals Board issued to a Federal agency becomes effective, the head of the department, agency, or instrumentality of the United States to which the order was issued can request a conference with the Administrator [40 C.F.R. § 22.31(e)].

EPA AND HUD REAL ESTATE NOTIFICATION AND DISCLOSURE RULE QUESTIONS AND ANSWERS

Adapted from
www.ct.gov/dph/lib/dph/environmental_health/lead/pdf/1018qa.pdf.
Please check with an attorney for the correct format and procedure for your state.

The Rule

What is the purpose of this rule and who is affected?
To protect the public from exposure to lead from paint, dust, and soil, Congress passed the Residential Lead-Based Paint Hazard Reduction Act of 1992, also known as Title X. Section 1018 of this law directed HUD and EPA to require disclosure of information on lead-based paint and lead-based paint hazards before the sale or lease of most housing built before 1978. The rule would ensure that purchasers and renters of housing built before 1978 receive the information necessary to protect themselves and their families from lead-based paint hazards.

When does the rule take effect?
The rule's effective date depends on the number of housing units owned.

- For owners of more than 4 dwelling units, the effective date is September 6, 1996.
- For owners of 4 or fewer dwelling units, the effective date is December 6, 1996.

Affected Housing

What type of housing is affected by this rule?
This rule applies to all housing defined as target housing, which includes most private housing, public housing, housing receiving federal assistance, and federally owned housing built before 1978.

What type of housing is not affected by this rule?
Housing that is not affected by this rule includes:

- 0-bedroom dwellings, such as lofts, efficiencies, and studios.
- Leases of dwelling units of 100 days or fewer, such as vacation homes or short-term rentals.
- Designated housing for the elderly and the handicapped unless children reside or are expected to reside there.
- Rental housing that has been inspected by a certified inspector and is found to be free of lead-based paint.

How does this rule apply to housing common areas such as stairwells, lobbies, and laundry rooms?

Common areas are those areas in multifamily housing structures that are used or are accessible to all occupants. The rule requires that sellers and lessors disclose available lead information about common areas so that families can be informed about preventive actions.

Why doesn't this rule affect housing built after 1978?

Congress did not extend the law to housing built after 1978 because the Consumer Product Safety Commission banned the use of lead-based paint in housing in 1978.

Is my home unsafe if it contains lead-based paint?

Approximately three-quarters of the nation's housing built before 1978 contains some lead-based paint. This paint, if properly managed and maintained, poses little risk. If allowed to deteriorate, lead from paint can threaten the health of occupants, especially children under 6 years old. If families and building owners are aware of the presence of lead-based paint and the proper actions to take, most lead-based paint hazards can be managed. The EPA pamphlet *Protect Your Family From Lead in Your Home* provides important information for families and home owners to help them identify when lead-based paint is likely to be a hazard and how to get their home checked.

Seller & Lessor Responsibilities

What if I'm selling target housing?

Property owners who sell target housing must:

- Disclose all known lead-based paint and lead-based paint hazards in the housing and any available reports on lead in the housing.
- Give buyers the EPA pamphlet *Protect Your Family from Lead in Your Home*.
- Include certain warning language in the contract as well as signed statements from all parties verifying that all requirements were completed.
- Retain signed acknowledgments for 3 years, as proof of compliance.
- Give buyers a 10-day opportunity to test the housing for lead.

What if I'm renting target housing?

Property owners who rent out target housing must:

- Disclose all known lead-based paint and lead-based paint hazards in the home and any available reports on lead in the housing.
- Give renters the EPA pamphlet *Protect Your Family From Lead in Your Home*.
- Include certain warning language in the lease as well as signed statements from all parties verifying that all requirements were completed.
- Retain signed acknowledgments for 3 years, as proof of compliance.

Am I required to give the EPA pamphlet *Protect Your Family From Lead in Your Home* to existing tenants?

No, but when tenants renew their leases, you must give them the pamphlet and any available reports. In other words, you must give them the same information that you are required to provide new tenants.

What if the buyers/renters don't speak English?

In cases where the buyer or renter signed a purchase or lease agreement in a language other than English, the rule requires that the disclosure language be provided in the alternate language. The EPA pamphlet *Protect Your Family From Lead in Your Home* is printed in English and Spanish and will be made available to the public. EPA and HUD are considering publishing the pamphlet in other languages as well.

Must I check my house for lead prior to sale?

No. The rule does not require that a seller conduct or finance an inspection or risk assessment. The seller, however, is required to provide the buyer a 10-day period to test for lead-based paint or lead-based paint hazards.

Is the seller required to remove any lead-based paint that is discovered during an inspection?

No. Nothing in the rule requires a building owner to remove lead-based paint or lead-based paint hazards discovered during an inspection or risk assessment. In addition, the rule does not prevent the two parties from negotiating hazard reduction activities as a contingency of the purchase and sale of the housing.

What if I know there is lead-based paint in my home?

If you know there is lead-based paint in your home, you are required to disclose this information to the buyer or renter along with any other available reports on lead.

What if the lessor knows that there is no lead-based paint in my rental housing?

If your rental housing has been found to be free of lead-based paint by a certified inspector, this rule does not apply. However, landlords seeking an exclusion to this rule must use state-certified inspectors. If your state does not have a certification program, you may use a certified inspector from another state. In addition, EPA is developing certification requirements for individuals and firms conducting lead-based paint inspections, risk assessments, and abatements.

Agent Responsibilities

What are my responsibilities as an agent?

Agents must ensure that:

- Sellers and landlords are made aware of their obligations under this rule.
- Sellers and landlords disclose the proper information to lessors, buyers, and tenants.

- Sellers give purchasers the opportunity to conduct an inspection.
- Lease and sales contracts contain the appropriate notification and disclosure language and proper signatures.

What is the responsibility of an agent if the seller or landlord fails to comply with this rule?

The agent is responsible for informing the seller or lessor of his or her obligations under this rule. In addition, the agent is responsible if the seller or lessor fails to comply. However, an agent is not responsible for information withheld by the seller or lessor.

Purchaser & Renter Rights

As a purchaser, am I required to conduct and finance an inspection?

No. The rule simply ensures that you have the opportunity to test for lead before purchase.

Can the inspection/risk assessment period be waived?

Yes. The inspection or risk assessment period can be lengthened, shortened, or waived by mutual written consent between the purchaser and the seller.

If I am renting, do I have the same opportunity to test for lead?

Under the law, the 10-day inspection period is limited to sales transactions, but nothing prevents the renter from negotiating with the lessor to allow time for an inspection before rental.

Where can I find a qualified professional to conduct an inspection?

State agencies can provide helpful information for locating qualified professionals in your area. The EPA pamphlet *Protect Your Family From Lead in Your Home* provides the phone numbers of these state agencies. It is important to verify the qualifications of individuals and firms before hiring them.

Must inspectors be certified?

Some cities and states have their own rules concerning inspector certification. These requirements, which may be administered at the state or federal level, may not be in place for several years. Once these requirements are in place, professionals who offer to perform lead-based paint inspections must be certified. The certification requirements that EPA is developing will ensure that inspectors engaged in lead-based paint activities have completed an EPA-certified training program or an EPA-approved state program. Meanwhile, EPA and HUD recommend that people inspect the qualifications and training of individuals and firms before hiring them to conduct risk assessments, inspections, or abatements.

Liability

Does this rule increase my liability for future lead poisoning on my property?
In some cases, disclosure may actually reduce the owner's liability since occupants may be able to prevent exposure from the beginning. Under this rule, however, sellers, landlords, or agents who fail to provide the required notices and information are liable for triple the amount of damages.

Are mortgage lenders liable under these rules if the seller or lessor fails to disclose?
Under the disclosure regulation, the rule does not identify mortgage lenders as liable parties. This rule does not affect other state and federal provisions regarding the obligations and responsibilities of lenders.

What if a seller or lessor fails to comply with these regulations?
A seller, lessor, or agent who fails to give the proper information can be sued for triple the amount of damages. In addition, they may be subject to civil and criminal penalties. Ensuring that disclosure information is given to home buyers and tenants helps all parties avoid misunderstandings before, during, and after sales and leasing agreements.

LEAD PAINT POISONING NOTICE FOR OWNER OR TENANT

(This notice should be sent via certified mail with a return receipt requested or by personal delivery whereby you get a signature from the tenant or property owner).

Date: _____

Sender of Notice's Name & Address:	Name & Address of Property Owner/Tenant being served this notice:
Phone:	Phone:

This notification is to inform you that the following has occurred or requires your attention:

❑ A child under the age of _____ years, or a pregnant woman, who resides at _____ has been diagnosed with a blood lead level of _____ or more on or before _____.

❑ The following areas need your immediate attention as they may contain lead:

The following areas have been found to contain peeling, chipping, flaking paint that is may be accessible to a child:

❑ Living Room ❑ Kitchen ❑ Bedroom ❑ Bathroom ❑ Dining Room
❑ Hallway ❑ Door Frame ❑ Porch ❑ Stairway ❑ Windows
❑ Exterior Walls ❑ Other Area(s) _____

The following areas have been found to contain structural defects:

❑ Living Room & Kitchen ❑ Bedroom ❑ Bathroom ❑ Dining Room
❑ Hallway ❑ Door Frame ❑ Porch ❑ Stairway ❑ Windows
❑ Exterior Walls ❑ Other Area(s) _____

Please list other Hazardous Conditions or areas:

_____

_____

I, _____Owner/Tenant of the aforementioned property hereby acknowledge having received this Lead Paint Poisoning Notice.

Signature _____ Date_____

LESSOR'S DISCLOSURE OF INFORMATION ON LEAD-BASED PAINT AND/OR LEAD-BASED PAINT HAZARDS

Lead Warning Statement

Housing built before 1978 may contain lead-based paint. Lead from paint, paint chips, and dust can pose health hazards if not managed properly. Lead exposure is especially harmful to young children and pregnant women. Before renting pre-1978 housing, lessors must disclose the presence of known lead based paint and/or lead-based paint hazards in the dwelling. Lessees must also receive a federally approved pamphlet on lead poisoning prevention.

Landlord's Disclosure

(a) Presence of lead-based paint and/or lead-based paint hazards (check (i) or (ii) below):

(i) _____ Known lead-based paint and/or lead-based paint hazards are present in the building (explain).

(ii) _____ Lessor has no knowledge of lead-based paint and/or lead-based paint hazards in the building.

(b) Records and reports available to the lessor (check (i) or (ii) below):

(i) _____ Lessor has provided the lessee with all available records and reports pertaining to lead-based paint and/or lead-based paint hazards in the building (list documents below).

(ii) _____ Lessor has no reports or records pertaining to lead-based paint and/or lead-based paint hazards in the building.

Tenant's Acknowledgment (initial)

(c) _____ Lessee has received copies of all information listed above.

(d) _____ Lessee has received the pamphlet *Protect Your Family from Lead in Your Home.*

Agent's Acknowledgment (initial)

(e) _____ Agent has informed the lessor of the lessor's obligations under 42 U.S.C. 4852d and is aware of his/her responsibility to ensure compliance.

Certification of Accuracy

The following parties have reviewed the information above and certify, to the best of their knowledge, that the information they have provided is true and accurate.

_____

Lessor   Date

_____

Lessee   Date

_____

Agent   Date

SELLER'S DISCLOSURE OF INFORMATION ON LEAD-BASED PAINT AND/OR LEAD-BASED PAINT HAZARDS

Lead Warning Statement

Every purchaser of any interest in residential real property on which a residential dwelling was built prior to 1978 is notified that such property may present exposure to lead from lead-based paint that may place young children at risk of developing lead poisoning. Lead poisoning in young children may produce permanent neurological damage, including learning disabilities, reduced intelligence quotient, behavioral problems, and impaired memory. Lead poisoning also poses a particular risk to pregnant women. The seller of any interest in residential real property is required to provide the buyer with any information on lead-based paint hazards from risk assessments or inspections in the seller's possession and notify the buyer of any known lead-based paint hazards. A risk assessment or inspection for possible lead-based paint hazards is recommended prior to purchase.

Seller's Disclosure

(a) Presence of lead-based paint and/or lead-based paint hazards (check (i) or (ii) below):

(i) _____ Known lead-based paint and/or lead-based paint hazards are present in the housing (explain).

_____

(ii) _____ Seller has no knowledge of lead-based paint and/or lead-based paint hazards in the housing.

(b) Records and reports available to the seller (check (i) or (ii) below):

(i) _____ Seller has provided the purchaser with all available records and reports pertaining to lead-based paint and/or lead-based paint hazards in the housing (list documents below).

_____

(ii) _____ Seller has no reports or records pertaining to lead-based paint and/or lead-based paint hazards in the housing.

Purchaser's Acknowledgment (initial)

(c) _____ Purchaser has received copies of all information listed above.

(d) _____ Purchaser has received the pamphlet *Protect Your Family from Lead in Your Home.*

(e) Purchaser has (check (i) or (ii) below):

(i) _____ received a 10-day opportunity (or mutually agreed upon period) to conduct a risk assessment or inspection for the presence of lead-based paint and/or lead-based paint hazards; or

(ii) _____ waived the opportunity to conduct a risk assessment or inspection for the presence of lead-based paint and/or lead-based paint hazards.

Agent's Acknowledgment (initial)

(f) _____ Agent has informed the seller of the seller's obligations under 42 U.S.C. 4852d and is aware of his/her responsibility to ensure compliance.

Certification of Accuracy

The following parties have reviewed the information above and certify, to the best of their knowledge, that the information they have provided is true and accurate.

_____   _____
Seller   Date

_____   _____
Purchaser   Date

_____   _____
Agent   Date

LEAD PAINT POISONING DISCLOSURE

Date: _____

This building was built before 1978 and has probably been painted with lead-based paint. Lead from paint, paint chips, and dust can pose health hazards, particularly to young children and pregnant women, if not managed properly. Lead poisoning in young children may produce permanent neurological damage, including learning disabilities, reduced intelligence quotient, behavioral problems, and impaired memory. Its effects may occur gradually and imperceptibly, often showing no obvious symptoms.

Lead-based paint that is in good condition is usually not a hazard. Children are at risk of getting lead poisoning if they ingest lead from paint chips, which are clearly visible, or lead dust, which is not always visible. Lead-based paint may also be a hazard when found on surfaces that children can chew or that receive a lot of wear-and-tear, such as windows and window sills, doors and doorframes, stairs, railings and banisters, and porches. Lead paints and primers may have been used in many places outdoors, such as on walls, fences, and porches. Lead from exterior house paint may be present in the soil around the outside of the building. The possibility of exposure to lead can be minimized by dusting window sills and other surfaces regularly with a damp cloth, and by preventing small children from chewing on painted surfaces or ingesting paint chips. Newspaper, pottery, furniture, and common household dust may also contain lead. Inform your family and any guests with small children about the danger of lead poisoning.

Your signature on this document is an acknowledgment that you understand the risk posed by lead-based paint in buildings constructed before 1978, and that you agree to hold us harmless of any possible problems that could result from lead-based paint, and any costs involved in diagnosis and treatment of such problems. This agreement includes all people who will be living with you in the building, those for whom you are responsible, and your guests.

Landlord:

____ Lead-based paint and/or lead-based paint hazards are known to be present in the building (explain):

_____

____ Landlord has no knowledge of lead-based paint and/or lead-based paint hazards in the building.

____ Landlord has provided the tenant with all available records and reports pertaining to lead-based paint and/or lead-based paint hazards in the building (list documents below).

_____

____ Landlord has no reports or records pertaining to lead-based paint and/or lead-based paint hazards in the building.

Tenant: (Initial below)

____ Tenant has received copies of all information listed above.

____ Tenant has received the pamphlet "Protect Your Family from Lead in Your Home."

Tenant: _____

Date: _____

Landlord: _____

Date: _____

Glossary

401(k): An investment plan sponsored by an employer that enables individuals to set aside pre-tax income for retirement or emergency purposes. 401(k) plans are provided by private corporations.

A

Accelerated Depreciation: A method of depreciation where the value of a property depreciates faster in the first few years after purchasing it.

Acceptance: An approval of a buyer's offer written by the seller.

Addendum: An addition or update for an existing contract between parties.

Administrative Costs: A percentage of the value of the assets under management, or a fixed annual dollar amount charged to manage an account.

Advisor: A broker or investment banker who represents an owner in a transaction and is paid a retainer and/or a performance fee once a financing or sales transaction has closed.

Amortization: The usual process of paying a loan's interest and principal via scheduled monthly payments.

Amortization Schedule: A chart or table which shows the percentage of each payment that will be applied toward principal and interest over the life of the mortgage and how the loan balance decreases until it reaches zero.

Amortization Tables: The mathematical tables that are used to calculate what a borrower's monthly payment will be.

Amortization Period: The number of months it will take to amortize the loan.

Application: The form a borrower must complete in order to apply for a mortgage loan, including information such as income, savings, assets, and debts.

Application Fee: A fee some lenders charge that may include charges for items such as property appraisal or a credit report unless those fees are included elsewhere.

Appraisal: The estimate of the value of a property on a particular date given by a professional appraiser, usually presented in a written document.

Appraisal Report: The written report presented by an appraiser regarding the value of a property.

Appraiser: A certified individual who is qualified by education, training, and experience to estimate the value of real and personal property.

Appreciation: An increase in the home's or property's value.

Arbitrage: The act of buying securities in one market and selling them immediately in another market in order to profit from the difference in price.

ARM index: A number that is publicly published and used as the basis for interest rate adjustments on an ARM.

As-Is Condition: A phrase in a purchase or lease contract in which the new tenant accepts the existing condition of the premises as well as any physical defects.

Assessed Value: The value placed on a home which is determined by a tax assessor in order to calculate a tax base.

Assessment: (1) The approximate value of a property. (2) A fee charged in addition to taxes in order to help pay for items such as water, sewer, street improvements, etc.

Asset: A property or item of value owned by an individual or company.

Assumption: The act of assuming the mortgage of the seller.

Assumption Fee: A fee charged to the buyer for processing new records when they are assuming an existing loan.

B

Balance Sheet: A statement that lists an individual's assets, liabilities and net worth.

Bankrupt: The state an individual or business is in if they are unable to repay their debt when it is due.

Bankruptcy: A legal proceeding where a debtor can obtain relief from payment of certain obligations through restructuring their finances.

Bid: The price or range an investor is willing to spend on whole loans or securities.

Binder: (1) A report describing the conditions of a property's title. (2) An early agreement between seller and buyer.

Book Value: The value of a property based on its purchase amount plus upgrades or other additions with d epreciation subtracted.

Broker: A person who serves as a go-between for a buyer and seller.

C

Cap: A limit on how much the monthly payment or interest rate is allowed to increase in an adjustable-rate mortgage.

Capital Gain: The amount of excess when the net proceeds from the sale of an asset are higher than its book value.

Capital Improvements: Expenses that prolong the life of a property or add new improvements to it.

Capitalization Rate: The percentage of return as it is estimated from the net income of a property.

Cash Flow: The amount of income an investor receives on a rental property after operating expenses and loan payments have been deducted.

Cashier's Check: A check the bank draws on its own resources instead of a depositor's account.

Closing: The final act of procuring a loan and title in which documents are signed between the buyer and seller and/or their respective representation, and all money, concerned in the contract, changes hands.

Closing Costs: The expenses that are related to the sale of real estate including loan, title, and appraisal fees and are beyond the price of the property itself.

Collection: The effort on the part of a lender, due to a borrower defaulting on a loan, which involves mailing and recording certain documents in the event that the foreclosure procedure must be implemented.

Commission: A compensation to salespeople that is paid out of the total amount of the purchase transaction.

Commitment: The agreement of a lender to make a loan with given terms for a specific period.

Comparable Sales: Also called Comps or Comparables. The recent selling prices of similar properties in the area that are used to help determine the market value of a property.

Condominium: A type of ownership in which all of the unit owners own the property, common areas, and buildings jointly, and have sole ownership in the unit to which they hold the title.

Contract: An agreement, either verbal or written, to perform or not to perform a certain thing.

Conventional Loan: A long-term loan from a nongovernmental lender that a borrower obtains for the purchase of a home.

Covenant: A written agreement, included in deeds or other legal documents, that defines the requirements for certain acts or use of a property.

Credit: An agreement in which a borrower promises to repay the lender at a later date and receives something of value in exchange.

Credit History: An individual's record that details his current and past financial obligations and performance.

Credit Rating: The degree of creditworthiness a person is assigned based on his credit history and current financial status.

Credit Report: An individual's record detailing an individual's credit, employment, and residence history used to determine the individual's creditworthiness.

Credit Score: Sometimes called a Credit Risk Score. The number contained in a consumer's credit report that represents a statistical summary of the information.

Creditor: A party to whom other parties owe money.

D

Debt: Any amount one party owes to another party.

Debt Service: The amount of money that is necessary to meet all interest and principal payments during a specific period.

Deed: A legal document that conveys property ownership to the buyer.

Default: The state that occurs when a borrow fails to fulfill a duty or take care of an obligation, such as making monthly mortgage payments.

Deposit: Also referred to as "Earnest Money." The funds that the buyer provides when offering to purchase property.

Depreciation: A decline in the value of property or an asset, often used as a tax deductible item.

Disclosure: A written statement, presented to a potential buyer, that lists information relevant to a piece of property, whether positive or negative.

Discretion: The amount of authority an adviser or manager is granted for investing and managing a client's capital.

Dividend: Distributions of cash or stock that stockholders receive.

Down Payment: The variance between the purchase price and the portion that the mortgage lender financed.

Due Diligence: The activities of a prospective purchaser or mortgager of real property for the purpose of confirming that the property is as represented by the seller and is not subject to environmental or other problems.

E

Equifax: One of the three primary credit-reporting bureaus.

Equity: The value of a property after existing liabilities have been deducted.

Escrow: A valuable item, money or documents deposited with a third party for delivery upon the fulfillment of a condition.

Escrow Account: Also referred to as an Impound Account. An account established by a mortgage lender or servicing company for the purpose of holding funds for the payment of items, such as homeowners insurance and property taxes.

Eviction: The legal removal of an occupant from a piece of property.

Exit strategy: An approach investors may use when they wish to liquidate all or part of their investment.

F

Fair Credit Reporting Act (FCRA): The federal legislation that governs the processes credit reporting agencies must follow.

Fair Housing Act: The federal legislation that prohibits the refusal to rent or sell to anyone based on race, color, religion, sex, family status, B268, or disability.

Fair Market Value: The highest price that a buyer would be willing to pay, and the lowest a seller would be willing to accept.

Fixed-Rate Mortgage: A loan with an unchanging interest rate over the life of the loan.

Fixture: Items that become a part of the property when they are permanently attached to the property.

Flat Fee: An amount of money that an adviser or manager receives for managing a portfolio of real estate assets.

Flood Insurance: A policy that is required in designated flood zones to protect against loss due to flood damage.

For Sale By Owner (FSBO): A method of selling property in which the property owner serves as the selling agent and directly handles the sales process with the buyer or buyer's agent.

Foreclosure: The legal process in which a lender takes over ownership of a property once the borrower is in default in a mortgage arrangement.

G

Gift: Money a buyer has received from a relative or other source.

Grace Period: A defined time period in which a borrower may make a loan payment after its due date without incurring a penalty.

Grant: To give or transfer an interest in a property by deed or other documented method.

Gross Income: The total income of a household before taxes or expenses have been subtracted.

H

Hazard Insurance: Also known as Homeowners' Insurance or Fire Insurance. A policy that provides coverage for damage from forces, such as fire and wind.

Home Equity Line: An open-ended amount of credit based on the equity a homeowner has accumulated.

Home Equity Loan: A type of loan that allows owners to borrow against the equity in their homes up to a limited amount.

Home Price: The price that a buyer and seller agree upon, generally based on the home's appraised market value.

Homeowners' Association Fees: The monthly payments that are paid to the homeowners' association for maintenance and communal expenses.

Housing and Urban Development (HUD): A federal agency that oversees a variety of housing and community development programs, including the FHA.

HVAC: Heating, Ventilating, and Air Conditioning.

I

Improvements: The upgrades or changes made to a building to improve its value or usefulness.

Insurance Binder: A temporary insurance policy that is implemented while a permanent policy is drawn up or obtained.

Interest Rate: The percentage that is charged for a loan.

Interest: The price that is paid for the use of capital.

Inventory: The entire space of a certain proscribed market without concern for its availability or condition.

Investment Property: A piece of real estate that generates some form of income.

J

Judgment: The decision a court of law makes.

L

Late Charge: The fee that is imposed by a lender when the borrower has not made a payment when it was due.

Late Payment: The payment made to the lender after the due date has passed.

Lease: A contract between a property owner and tenant that defines payments and conditions under which the tenant may occupy the real estate for a given period of time.

Leasehold: The limited right to inhabit a piece of real estate held by a tenant.

Lender: A bank or other financial institution that offers home loans.

Leverage: The process of increasing the return on an investment by borrowing some of the funds at an interest rate less than the return on the project.

Liabilities: A borrower's debts and financial obligations, whether long- or short-term.

Liability Insurance: A type of policy that protects owners against negligence, personal injury, or property damage claims.

Lien: A claim put by one party on the property of another as collateral for money owed.

Line of Credit: An amount of credit granted by a financial institution up to a specified amount for a certain period of time to a borrower.

Loan: An amount of money that is borrowed and usually repaid with interest.

Loan Application: A document that presents a borrower's income, debt, and other obligations to determine credit worthiness, as well as some basic information on the target property.

Loan Application Fee: A fee lenders charge to cover expenses relating to reviewing a loan application.

Loan Officer: An official representative of a lending institution who is authorized to act on behalf of the lender within specified limits.

Loan Origination: The process of obtaining and arranging new loans.

Loan Origination Fee: A fee lenders charge to cover the costs related to arranging the loan.

Loan Servicing: The process a lending institution goes through for all loans it manages. This involves processing payments, sending statements, managing the escrow/impound account, providing collection services on delinquent loans, ensuring that insurance and property taxes are made on the property, handling pay-offs and assumptions, as well as various other services.

Loan Term: The time, usually expressed in years, that a lender sets in which a buyer must pay a mortgage.

Lock-In: A commitment from a lender to a borrower to guarantee a given interest rate for a limited amount of time.

Lot: One of several contiguous parcels of a larger piece of land.

M

Market Value: The price a property would sell for at a particular point in time in a competitive market.

Modification: An adjustment in the terms of a loan agreement.

Mortgage: An amount of money that is borrowed to purchase a property using that property as collateral.

Mortgage Banker: A financial institution that provides home loans using its own resources, often selling them to investors such as insurance companies or Fannie Mae.

Mortgage Broker: An individual that matches prospective borrowers with lenders that the broker is approved to deal with.

Mortgage Insurance (MI): A policy, required by lenders on some loans, that covers the lender against certain losses that are incurred as a result of a default on a home loan.

Mortgagee: The financial institution that lends money to the borrower.

N

Net Cash Flow: The total income generated by an investment property after expenses have been subtracted.

Net Operating Loss (NOL): When your expenses subtracted from your gross income are a negative number.

O

Offer: A term that describes a specified price or spread to sell whole loans or securities.

Option: A condition in which the buyer pays for the right to purchase a property within

Owner Financing: A transaction in which the property seller agrees to finance all or part of the amount of the purchase.

P

Partial Payment: An amount paid that is not large enough to cover the normal monthly payment on a mortgage loan.

Performance: The changes each quarter in fund or account values that can be explained by investment income, realized or unrealized appreciation, and the total return to the investors before and after investment management fees.

Personal Property: Any items belonging to a person that is not real estate.

PITI: Principal, Interest, Taxes, Insurance. The items that are included in the monthly payment to the lender for an impounded loan, as well as mortgage insurance.

Point: Also referred to as a Discount Point. A fee a lender charges to provide a lower interest rate, equal to one percent of the amount of the loan.

Pre-Approval: The complete analysis a lender makes regarding a potential borrower's ability to pay for a home as well as a confirmation of the proposed amount to be borrowed.

Prepayment: The money that is paid to reduce the principal balance of a loan before the date it is due.

Prime Rate: The best interest rate reserved for a bank's preferred customers.

Principal: The amount of money originally borrowed in a mortgage, before interest is included and with any payments subtracted.

Pro Rata: The proportionate amount of expenses per tenant for the property's maintenance and operation.

Prohibited Transaction: Certain transactions that may not be performed between a pension plan and a party in interest, such as the following: the sale, exchange or lease of any property; a loan or other grant of credit; and furnishing goods or services.

Promissory Note: A written agreement to repay the specific amount over a certain period of time.

Property Tax: The tax that must be paid on private property.

Purchase Agreement: The written contract the buyer and seller both sign defining the terms and conditions under which a property is sold.

R

Rating: A figure that represents the credit quality or creditworthiness of securities.

Real Estate Agent: An individual who is licensed to negotiate and transact the real estate sales.

Realtor: A real estate agent or broker who is an active member of a local real estate board affiliated with the National Association of Realtors.

Rehab: Short for Rehabilitation. Refers to an extensive renovation intended to extend the life of a building or project.

Real Estate Investment Trust (REIT): A trust corporation that combines the capital of several investors for the purpose of acquiring or providing funding for real estate.

Renewal Option: A clause in a lease agreement that allows a tenant to extend the term of a lease.

Rent: The fee paid for the occupancy and/or use of any rental property or equipment.

Replacement Cost: The projected cost by current standards of constructing a building that is equivalent to the building being appraised.

Return on Investments: The percentage of money that has been gained as a result of certain investments.

S

Second Mortgage: A secondary loan obtained upon a piece of property.

Security: The property or other asset that will serve as a loan's collateral.

Security Deposit: An amount of money a tenant gives to a landlord to secure the performance of terms in a lease agreement.

Separate Account: A relationship in which a single pension plan sponsor is used to retain an investment manager or adviser under a stated investment policy exclusively for that sponsor.

Subcontractor: A contractor who has been hired by the general contractor, often specializing in a certain required task for the construction project.

Subdivision: The most common type of housing development created by dividing a larger tract of land into individual lots for sale or lease.

T

Taking: Similar to condemning, or any other interference with rights to private property, but a physical seizure or appropriation is not required.

Tenant (Lessee): A party who rents a piece of real estate from another by way of a lease agreement.

Term: The length that a loan lasts or is expected to last before it is repaid.

Title: The legal written document which provides someone ownership in a piece of real estate.

Title Company: A business that determines that a property title is clear and that provides title insurance.

Title Insurance: A type of policy that is issued to both lenders and buyers to cover loss due to property ownership disputes that may arise at a later date.

Total Loan Amount: The basic amount of the loan plus any additional financed closing costs.

Trustee: A fiduciary who oversees property or funds on behalf of another party.

U

Underwriter: A company, usually an investment banking firm, that is involved in a guarantee that an entire issue of stocks or bonds will be purchased.

Underwriting: The process during which lenders analyze the risks a particular borrower presents and set appropriate conditions for the loan.

Underwriting Fee: A fee that mortgage lenders charge for verifying the information on the loan application and making a final decision on approving the loan.

Use: The particular purpose for which a property is intended to be employed.

V

Vacancy Rate: The percentage of space that is available to rent.

Vacant Space: Existing rental space that is presently being marketed for lease minus space that is available for sublease.

Vested: Having the right to draw on a portion or on all of a pension or other retirement fund.

W

Working Drawings: The detailed blueprints for a construction project that comprise the contractual documents which describe the exact manner in which a project is to be built.

Write-Down: A procedure used in accounting when an asset's book value is adjusted downward to reflect current market value more accurately.

Z

Zoning: The act of dividing a city or town into particular areas and applying laws and regulations regarding the architectural design, structure, and intended uses of buildings within those areas.

Index

Relax.
It's **rented.**

*Manage your investments,
not your properties.*

Rented.com can help you find the right
manager for your investment property.

With a free network of more than 700 professional
property managers, Rented.com makes it easy to **find,
compare, and choose the right manager** to take care of
everything from cleaning to maintenance—for free.

rented.com
+1 (844) 736-8334
info@rented.com